The art of living in peace: guide to education for a culture of peace

In this series

The art of living in peace

Guide to education for a culture of peace

Pierre Weil
Rector of the International Holistic University
of the City of Peace Foundation in Brasilia
UNIPAIX

Cultures of Peace | UNESCO PUBLISHING
UNIPAIX

Published in 2002 by the United Nations Educational,
Scientific and Cultural Organization,
7, place de Fontenoy, 75352 Paris 07 SP
Typeset by Gérard Prosper
Printed by Imprimerie Landais

ISBN Unipaix 2-9600321-1-X
ISBN UNESCO 92-3-103804-4

Preface

These are times in which humanity is struggling in a complex of crises, often interrelated, the outcome of which could pose real challenges for its survival. Protection of the environment, sustainable development, the growth of the world population, the promotion of democracy, respect for human rights, security and the fight against international terrorism are all major issues for which there are no easy solutions. It is essential to think on a global scale and advance universal values with which everyone will be able to identify. 'Planetary ethics', 'global citizenship' and 'holistic thinking' will then be able to emerge, founded on humanistic and cultural values, on a realistic view of what is required to conserve our planet, and on recognition of the need for all peoples to live together.

Within the United Nations system, UNESCO is working to construct the defences of peace in the minds of men, in particular through education, as emphasized in its Constitution, adopted in 1946. This mission is still just as relevant. Wars – whether local or international – are legion and the threat of a global conflict has not been wholly averted. Conflicts are very often based on prejudice and on doctrines advocating inequality of races and individuals, sometimes based on misinterpretation of religious texts. Today, as yesterday, education for peace is absolutely essential and is a long-term undertaking.

Education for peace and non-violence is a challenge. Age-old customs, prejudices and traditions sometimes inhibit initiatives or prevent the adoption of new attitudes and ways of thinking. The road is long and the search must be unremitting if we wish to see the emergence of a renewed awareness and a responsible form of citizenship for a future of peace.

For more than ten years, 'The Art of Living in Peace' has been successfully used in seminars on education for a culture of peace, aimed at teachers, trainers and young people, in several countries throughout the world. UNESCO is particularly proud to have contributed to the spread of the method that it presents, which has lost none of its relevance and effectiveness, and would like to pay tribute to the author, Professor Pierre Weil, Rector of the International Holistic University of Brasilia and Chairman of the City of Peace of Foundation, to whom UNESCO awarded its Education for Peace Prize (honourable mention) in 2000.

This publication hopes to assist in making known, throughout the world of formal and non-formal education, methods and practices of conflict resolution and prevention. UNESCO is contributing in this way to the International Decade for a Culture of Peace and Non-Violence for the Children of the World, proclaimed by the United Nations for the period 2001–2010.

Acknowledgements

This book, previously published as a document by UNESCO in 1990, was revised and updated for issue in its present form by the author. Its publication was made possible by the support of the UNIPAIX Associations for Europe, France and Belgium and, in particular, by the outstanding work of Dominique Rémi.

An essential contribution was provided by the UNESCO Division for the Promotion of Quality Education, which funded this edition together with the Minister-President of the Communauté Wallonie-Bruxelles of Belgium (whose remit includes culture and education).

Transdev, a group that provides public service transport to people in some one hundred towns and regions of the world, has also provided support for this edition. The services rendered every day by Transdev employees constitute a contribution to peace in the towns, suburbs and regions which they cover. In the face of the specific problems posed by rising levels of violence, Transdev has developed over the last few years an original approach that emphasizes conflict prevention, training for employees in communication skills, the provision of public services in difficult neighbourhoods, the employment of young people from such neighbourhoods in work teams and the promotion of civic values. By proposing an alternative to approaches based on security concerns, Transdev is contributing to solidarity, responsiveness and generosity among citizens, fundamental aspects of UNESCO's Manifesto 2000.

The author, Pierre Weil, to whom UNESCO offers its thanks, is responsible for the presentation of the facts contained in this book and for the opinions expressed therein, which are not necessarily those of UNESCO and do not commit the Organization.

Contents

Appendices

Introduction

During the forty years' existence of the United Nations, and UNESCO in particular, a great deal of research has been carried out into the causes of war and the means to establish peace in the world.

All over the world, in parallel with this research, a curriculum for teaching peace is being developed, to a large extent inspired by the work and official statements of these international organizations.

The time has come to attempt to form an overview of this research and these teaching methods in order both to understand them intellectually and to trigger a profound change in the attitudes and behaviour of human beings.

A new consciousness is developing in the minds of many of our fellow human beings, together with a change of paradigm which inspires a new way of looking at science, philosophy, art and education. A new holistic vision of the world is in the process of being born.

It is important that educators for peace the world over are aware of this development and its implications for all of us, and that this information is made available in language that is simple, and as accessible as possible.

Moreover, for educators to be in tune with the times and to be able to respond to the demands of current events, we must provide them with the educational methods for transforming consciousness, starting with their own, so that they themselves can be examples of peace and harmony. Indeed, how can we change other people, if we do not start with ourselves?

These then are the essential aims of this book, whose contents – which are a provisional synthesis – are our entire responsibility. It does not commit UNESCO as an institution, although it derives a lot of its inspiration from UNESCO's work.

As the subject is education for peace for educators, the methods described here are primarily aimed at adults. As for their adaptation to meet the needs of youth and children, this question must be studied later, bearing in mind, of course, the efforts currently under way in the world.

Introduction
to the second edition

Ten years have passed since UNESCO first published this work. Here now is a second edition, revised and expanded to include certain basic documents.

A great many people have been able to attend the seminar on 'the art of living in peace' seminar, and have expressed their thanks to its leader, saying that they found what they were looking for or that the seminar marked the beginning of a real change in their way of being.

The growing success of this method is not only due to the fact that it addresses both heart and mind. As the UNESCO Prize for Peace Education Jury has pointed out, it is also a synthesis of Western and Eastern teaching methods, which means that it unites the male functions linked to the left-hand side of the brain with the female ones linked to the right-hand side.

During the past ten years, violence has increased around the world to such an extent that the very recent concept of peace education has managed to make headway, despite the imposing obstacle represented by the most common definition of peace, that is to say, peace as the absence of war.

The interactive triangle we have introduced in the domain of peace education has contributed significantly to diminishing the reductive influence of this concept. It is based on a holistic vision according to which the art of living in peace must be envisaged as the result of a process with three inseparable and interdependent dimensions: peace with oneself, with others and with nature.

This new model has provided practical guidance for all the Brasilia programmes of UNIPAZ, a holistic university for peace with offshoots in Buenos Aires, Lisbon, Paris, Brussels and even in Israel, where Arab and Jewish educators followed the seminar on the art of living in peace together.

In France, UNESCO's Education Sector carried out an initial experiment in spring 1999 at the World Heritage site of the Royal Saltworks of Arc-et-Senans. It was aimed at adolescents in risk situations, and organized in conjunction with the French National Commission for UNESCO, the World Heritage Centre (which provided the funding), the AFI (reception, training, reintegration) association of Bourg-en-Bresse, the European branch of UNIPAIX (the European association for peace education) and the Nicolas-Ledoux Institute as part of the 'Universe-City' project established by the International Transdisciplinary Centre for Peace Education (CITEP). The seminar on the art of living in peace was used as the model. A profound transformation was observed by the educators and given enthusiastic expression by the participants.

The action of this first seminar has also been reinforced in the last few years by a two-year training course in the method, a practical application of the principles of the 'Delors Report', which was recommended by UNESCO. The course teaches an art of living that harmoniously combines knowing, doing, being and living together.

Thus, the art of living in peace has shown itself to be an excellent tool for helping the world to transform the current culture of war into a culture of peace at the dawn of the third millennium and of the first decade of the twenty-first century, proclaimed by the United Nations General Assembly 'International Decade for a Culture of Peace and Non-Violence for the Children of the World'.

Preliminary considerations on the methodology

This book is written in simple language that is easily understood by the main cultures on Earth and attempts to bring together theoretical data with recommended practical techniques that can be used in education for peace.

Therefore, each description of the conclusions drawn from hypotheses and research about peace, about the obstacles that prevent its realization and the methods that encourage its development or awakening, is accompanied by methodological curriculum recommendations for short-, medium- and long-term education.

Short-term programme

This refers to a 15- to 20-hour programme that allows participants to become aware of the problem. A prototype workshop of this kind has been initiated by the City of Peace Foundation and the International Holistic University of Brasilia, under the title 'The Art of Living in Peace'. It serves as an introduction to a training programme for educators and teachers of peace, but also – and above all – it is meant for the general public the world over and will be used during UNESCO's regional seminars.

Medium-term programme

This refers to a 3- to 6-month programme that goes more deeply into the contents of the short-term workshop.

Long-term programme

This refers to a programme that provides an in-depth education in this art as it should be developed in all the schools of the world.

Our premise is that this education should start with the educators themselves. Through the example of their inner peace and their
ability to radiate it and develop it in others, it will be possible to go
beyond intellectual and academic transmission which is the first phase
in a worldwide process, the aim of which is to bring about a culture of
peace.

UNESCO's proclamation of 2000 as the 'International Year for
the Culture of Peace' bears witness to this movement as does the United
Nations decision to proclaim the first decade of the third millennium,
2001–2010, 'International Decade for the Promotion of a Culture of
Non-violence and Peace for the Children of the World' in response to
an appeal signed by all the Nobel Peace Prize winners, first made to
them in 1997.

We consider that this type of education should begin with the
educators themselves. By setting an example with their own inner peace
and passing it on in their interactions with others, they will be able to go
beyond the mere teaching of concepts that is typical of today's world.
Each part of this book may be considered as an educational module. For
each module you will find:

- A summary of the principal aspects of the subject and the current
  situation.
- A reference list of essential sources.
- A list of recommended educational methods.
- A short list of suggested reading.

Method of education

The contents of this programme are in line with the recommendations
and embody the spirit of the following:

- The Preamble to UNESCO's Constitution.
- The Recommendation Concerning Education for International
  Understanding, Co-operation and Peace and Education Relating
  to Human Rights and Fundamental Freedoms, 1974.
- The Seville Statement on Violence, 1986.
- The Venice Declaration on Science and the Boundaries of
  Knowledge, 1987.
- The Vancouver Declaration, 1989.
- The Preparatory Meeting to the International Experts' Confer-
  ence of Yamoussoukro on Peace in the Minds of Men, 1989.
- The Yamoussoukro Declaration on Peace in the Minds of Men,
  1989.

- Report to UNESCO of the International Commission on Education for the Twenty-first Century: 'Learning: The Treasure Within', 1996.

As a method of education, we recommend alternating between theory and practical action in real life. We start with theory, in order to prepare people to absorb the real-life experience. After they have had the experience, we return to the theory and examine what has taken place, so that we can draw some conclusions or even make some decisions with regard to daily life. This also allows people to share their experiences with others taking the course.

The techniques employed are inspired by a variety of sources and cultures, and this in itself serves to increase international understanding. We would like to mention the following sources in particular:

- 'Active' methods of education from Europe.
- Explanatory methods common to all cultures.
- Dialectical methods as practised by all major cultures.
- Various types of yoga originating from India, Nepal and Tibet.
- Tai-chi as practised in China.
- Martial arts as practised in Japan and China.
- Dance from all over the world.
- Music as a non-verbal international language.
- The graphic arts.
- Theatre and role-playing.
- Educational and traditional games.
- Mass media techniques and their educational role in the world: the press, radio, television, advertising, propaganda.
- Training techniques used in the business world.
- Non-violent methods inspired from India.
- Conflict management techniques originating from various European and American psychological and sociological schools of thought.
- Practices for awakening wisdom from, among others, African, Buddhist, Christian, Hindu, Indian, Jewish, Muslim and shamanistic traditions.
- Group and individual psychotherapy techniques.

While respecting the diversity of these sources, it is important gradually to try and develop a holistic, interdisciplinary and transdisciplinary approach to education for peace. This point will be further developed later.

We shall start with an introduction to the theoretical aspects of our programme. This is necessary since it underlines the fact that a new paradigm is emerging: the importance of becoming aware of it, and its crucial influence on the development of a new approach to education for peace.

These preliminary thoughts will lead us to the heart of the matter: the aforementioned new method of education for peace –'The Art of Living in Peace' – inspired by one of the fundamental models developed by the International Holistic University of Brasilia.

The content of the second part of the book is the fruit of around twenty years of research. It results from refining a method of awareness-awakening that had the primary objective of helping individuals find their own inner peace and its relation to certain states of consciousness. In addition, this method demonstrates how the reality in which we live is a function of our state of mind at any given moment. This research was carried out by the Department of Psychology at the Federal University of Minas Gerais, Brazil, under the auspices of the Chair of Transpersonal Psychology. We originally called this research 'Cosmodrama' and later 'Dance of Life'.

This led to the current programme entitled 'The Art of Living Life' which lasts two years and is organized in the form of eight modules, namely:

- 'The Art of Living in Peace.'
- 'The Art of Living Aware.'
- 'The Art of Living Fulfilled.'
- 'The Art of Living in Harmony.'
- 'The Art of Living with Conflict.'
- 'The Art of Living with Nature.'
- 'The Art of Living with the Passing of Time.'
- 'And Life Goes On . . . '

This is the fruit of a synthesis of the schools of thought and the methods mentioned above.

The 'Art of Living in Peace' programme is made up, to some extent, of a selection of the techniques most appropriate to achieving its aims.

The first part of this programme is specifically aimed at educators, while the second part is meant for everyone in general. However, it is absolutely necessary, for reasons we give at the beginning of the second part of the book, that future educators using this method should take part in the 'Art of Living in Peace' training.

We shall now start by presenting the main theories that give rise to this new vision of education for peace.

The paradigm shift in science and its influence on education for peace

People interpret the words 'education' and 'peace' in several different ways according to their various points of view. These perspectives and differences in interpretation are mainly due to the extremely important influence of the Newtonian-Cartesian paradigm that has led human knowledge and our perception of the world into such a state of frag-mentation and – as far as science is concerned – into such a degree of specialization that we have lost contact with what is essential.

According to this perspective, the world is a collection of solid elements related to each other by structures and systems ruled by mechanical laws. Such a vision has enabled humanity to make remark-able scientific discoveries and develop technological applications that have led to a level of material well-being previously unknown in our his-tory. But it is also true that this world view has generated a crisis of fragmentation that has reached the point of endangering the survival of all life forms on the planet. We have arbitrarily cut up the world into territories which nations consider their sole property. We have divided knowledge into science, philosophy, art and religion. Each of these fields has in turn been subdivided into countless others, turning our univer-sities into veritable 'towers of Babel'. We ourselves, as human beings, have been split into body, emotions, mind and intuition.

It is exactly such divisions that underlie all the different interpret-ations of what peace is, as well as of what hinders or brings peace about. This world view is also, of course, one of the main reasons why peace was lost in the first place. To show how peace is destroyed and how it can be rebuilt is precisely the aim of *The Art of Living in Peace*. In addi-tion, the fragmented world view has created different and often oppos-ing perspectives and methods in the field of education.

We are witnesses to a transformation of our view of reality, to the birth of a new interdisciplinary and transdisciplinary paradigm that corresponds to a new vision of the world and of life. This new view, accompanied by a change in consciousness, is of a holistic nature. It is important that we are clearly aware of this transformation and of its considerable consequences for the subject of education for peace.

According to this point of view, which has arisen from the meeting of quantum physics with transpersonal psychology and the wisdom of the great spiritual traditions,[1] the systems of the universe are all formed from the same energy.[2] Coming from a space that we know is not empty but is made of a potential void which cannot be separated from the energy itself.[3] From this point of view any kind of duality or fragmentation is seen as a product of the human mind whose essential quality is precisely to classify, divide and fragment, and then to establish relationships between these tiny parts.

Table 1. The non-fragmentary vision of energy.
The forms of manifestation of energy and corresponding sciences

HUMANS	Form of manifestation of energy	Body	Emotion	Mind
	Corresponding sciences	Anatomy	Physiology	Psychology
SOCIETY	Form of manifestation of energy	Housing and economy	Social life	Culture
	Corresponding sciences	Economics	Sociology	Anthropology
NATURE	Form of manifestation of energy	Matter	Life	Information
	Corresponding sciences	Physics	Biology	Computer science

1. This meeting of disciplines is the objective of the recommendations of the Declaration of Venice, issued under the aegis of UNESCO. See *Science and the Boundaries of Knowledge*, Paris, UNESCO, 1987.
2. S. Lupasco, *Les Trois Matières*, Paris, Julliard, 1960.
3. G. Norel, *Histoire de la Matière et de la Vie, Les Transformations de l'Energie et de l'Evolution*, Paris, Maloine, 1984 (Collection Recherches Interdisciplinaires).

Energy has three basic forms: matter, life and information. These forms are studied by the three main branches of science: physics, biology and computer science which should be no more separated than the three human sciences, anatomy (body), physiology (life) and psychology (consciousness), or the three social sciences, anthropology (culture), sociology (social and political life) and economics (production and consumption). (See Table 1.)

We are now going to examine how the two perspectives and paradigms we have been discussing influence ideas related to education and to peace.

First of all, what is peace?

Chapter 1

Peace

A fragmentary vision of peace

A fragmentary vision of reality implies a separation between subject and object, 'object' being taken as all the things, persons or ideas which constitute the way in which most human beings currently see the universe in its relative dimension. By perceiving a subject-object duality, the subject perceives the object as separate from him just as he sees objects as separate from one another. This leads to what we shall call the 'fantasy of separation', which in turn leads to a fragmented view of peace.

According to this view we can identify two kinds of peace: external peace, or peace of the 'object', and internal peace, or peace of the 'subject'. Let us consider these two aspects.

Peace as a phenomenon external to ourselves

From this point of view, peace is a cultural, judicial, political, social and socio-economic phenomenon. The result is that peace is considered to belong to the area of the social sciences, which indeed have made an effective contribution to research into war and peace. The study of conflicts was born from this perspective.[1]

We can also make two further distinctions: peace seen as an absence of violence or war, and peace seen as a state of harmony.

Peace seen as the absence of violence or war

This view indicates the need for some kind of treatment of conflict and its causes, and general disarmament. In the case of the former, peace

---

1.   R. Bosc, *Sociologie de la Paix*, Paris, Spes, 1965.

would be the result of dealing with conflict, that is to say of the dissolution or transformation of the causes of the conflict. In the latter case, peace would be achieved by the elimination of the destructive aspects of conflict, i.e. violence and war, for some people conflict in itself presents some constructive dialectical aspects and evolutionary opportunities. Conflict is resolved through a search for consensus, which is one of the present concerns of UNESCO.[2]

Lawyers would insist that the solution to conflict depends upon the transformation of the judicial concept of a 'fair war' into that of the right to peace or, in other words, the transformation of the law of force into the force of the law.[3] This concept validates the role of international courts in resolving conflicts based upon a fundamental legal principle: the right of human beings to live in peace.

We also have to work on preventing conflict. The Declaration of Human Rights addresses this need, complemented by the Declaration of Human Responsibilities. (See Appendix 3.)

There is also a military assertion, which has existed since the dawn of time, that 'if you want peace, you must prepare for war' – a principle that is taught and developed in military academies. It demonstrates a fundamental and important paradox: that the basis and role of armed forces is not to fight wars but to maintain peace by using force. This paradox reaches its culmination in the present form of the peace-keeping forces of the United Nations.

The opposing view would insist that 'if you want peace, you should prepare for peace'. This perspective is responsible for efforts towards disarmament, begun during the era of the League of Nations, and aimed at the demobilization of armed forces. It is important to note that this latter idea can only be successfully put into practice if it is done on a totally multilateral basis – in other words, if it is undertaken by every nation without exception. Otherwise we run the risk of seeing one nation that is still armed dominate the others which have all disarmed. This is the main argument used by the heads of national armed forces to maintain and even develop their organizations.

Another perspective, the political one, shows how competition and nationalism constitute an important factor in war. The official

2.   Amadou-Mahtar M'Bow et al., *Consensus and Peace*, Paris, UNESCO, 1980.

3.   B. B. Ferencz and Ken Keyes, *Planethood: The Key to Your Future*, Preface by Robert Muller, Love Line Books, 1991.

solution to this is the establishment of a world government,[4] for which the League of Nations and later the United Nations represent a preparatory phase.

Peace seen as a state of harmony and brotherhood between people and nations

According to this second approach, the state of peace would be the result of direct and constructive work done in groups and societies. It emphasizes the education of societies by means of the mass media, with a change of public opinion at an intellectual level and of collective attitudes at a practical level. This approach, which brings together education and the mass media, is also one of the main focuses of UNESCO's work.[5]

The above two perspectives may be considered as belonging to a single category which we can call social ecology.

It is possible to extend the second perspective peace as a state of harmony – to nature and the planet itself. This broader definition conforms to the recent recommendations of UNESCO to include environmental problems with those of security and peace.[6] A new conception of security has been born, as shown by the Brundtland Report.[7] Thus, peace is linked to the ecology of the planet. Now let us move on to look at the idea of peace of the 'subject' or inner peace.

Peace seen as an inner state, a state of mind or 'peace in the human mind'

The idea of peace as an 'inner state of being' corresponds to the contents of the preamble to UNESCO's Constitution which states that 'since wars begin in the minds of men, it is in the minds of men that the defences of peace must be constructed'.[8] This concept could be called 'inner' or 'personal' ecology.

---

4.   A world constitutive assembly, held in Innsbruck, Austria, adopted a constitution for the federation of the planet. A congress was organized in Tours in 1990.
5.   UNESCO, *Media Education*, Paris, UNESCO, 1985.
6.   UNESCO, *Recommendations Concerning Education for International Understanding, Co-operation and Peace and Education relating to Human Rights and Fundamental Freedoms*, Paris, UNESCO, 1974; UNESCO, Yamoussoukro Declaration on Peace in the Minds of Men, Paris, UNESCO, 1989.
7.   G. H. Brundtland et al., *Our Common Future*, Oxford/New York, OUP, 1987 (Part III, Chap. 11).
8.   *UNESCO Constitution*, Paris, UNESCO.

Although often quoted, this preamble is rarely put into practice in real life, as shown by a short study published in the late 1980.[9] This study is based on information provided by UNESCO[10] and underlines the following facts: of the 310 institutions dedicated to education and research on peace, only 24 (5%) of the subjects taught related to inner peace, while maybe up to 14% of research was focused on this area.

Therefore, it is completely justifiable that the budget should include a programme entitled 'Peace in the Minds of Men' in the future. 'Since wars begin "in the minds of men", as stated in UNESCO's constitution, it is up to UNESCO and the schools all over the world to put an end to the beginning of war.'[11]

It was in accordance with this perspective that the Yamoussoukro Declaration on 'Peace in the Minds of Men' was written.[12]

One of the prophecies in the Bible states that swords will be beaten into ploughshares. It is possible to interpret this statement symbolically: it is within each human being that aggression and violence, represented by the sword, must be transformed into an energy of peace, represented by the ploughshare.

Some more or less successful efforts towards general disarmament on an exterior level may lead us to believe that this is all that is needed to establish peace. We have already mentioned this idea, when we were discussing peace viewed simply as an absence of conflict. Let us look at it again in connection with this prophecy: even if we destroy all our weapons, right down to the last gun – in other words, if we get rid of all the swords – unless we transform our inner selves, we shall still fight one another with our ploughshares. . . . Besides, can we not think that this is precisely what is happening when we look at the increase in violence and crime today in countries where, nevertheless, there is no more war?

As in the case where peace is seen as a phenomenon that is external to man, we are again faced with two different theories.

Peace as a result of the absence or dissolution of inner psychic conflicts
This is a psychotherapeutic concept. It is in eliminating the conflict between the ego and superego, between the heart and the mind, or

9.   *Peace in the Spirit of Man. A Forgotten Basic Principle of UNESCO.* IPRA, Congrès International, 1988.

10.   UNESCO–Berg, *World Directory of Peace Research and Training Institutions*, Paris, UNESCO, 1988.

11.   Robert Muller, speech given as a co-winner of UNESCO's Peace Education Award, UNESCO, 20 September 1989.

12.   See *Yamoussoukro Declaration*, op. cit.

between the intuition and the heart, for example, that it is possible to re-establish inner peace.

Peace as a state of inner harmony

This is a result of inner work that involves a non-fragmented vision of reality on the intellectual level, a detachment from any sort of concept, being or object. It comes from the birth of a 'natural' wisdom, which is bound up with altruistic love. It is a spiritual concept, linked to the great spiritual traditions of humanity,[13] and also to recent research in transpersonal psychology.[14]

We would like to point out in passing that we see here one of the results of the fragmentation of knowledge that characterizes the established paradigm, in that psychology has become separated from the spiritual traditions.

In conclusion, we can say that the fragmented vision of peace leads us to reductionist ideas which in themselves are an expression of the over-specialization and fragmentation of knowledge. Thus we are faced with various incompatible definitions.

A holistic vision of peace

A new vision of peace, the holistic vision is a non-fragmented vision. It will come about as a result of an approach which takes into account all the different points of view. Thus, a holistic vision of peace implies a non-fragmentary theory of space-energy in which energy manifests itself in the form of matter, life and information.

It is an approach that takes into account human beings, society and the natural world combining inner or personal ecology, social ecology and planetary ecology. These three aspects are intimately linked and constantly interacting. From this perspective peace is concurrently an inner state of consciousness arising from personal tranquillity, a state of social accord dependent upon an ability to solve conflicts peacefully, and a state of harmony with nature (see Table 2).

So we cannot have true peace at a personal level if we know that poverty and violence hold sway at the social level, or that the natural world threatens to destroy us because we are destroying it.

13.   Krishnamurti, *The First and Last Freedom*, Foreword by Aldous Huxley, Harper/ Collins.

14.   Pierre Weil, *L'Homme Sans Frontières*, Paris, L'Espace Bleu, 1989.

The holistic vision or consciousness implies a progressive broad-ening of consciousness. It begins with a personal awareness and dissolu-tion of egocentric aspects and a progression towards a social conscious-ness, although still an anthropocentric one – in other words seen from an exclusively human viewpoint. As and when society realizes the extent of its dependence on the planet and all its life forms, social conscious-ness will evolve into planetary consciousness. Even then this will still be to some extent geocentric, with its perspective somewhat limited to our planet, regarding it as the centre of the universe.

The holistic vision, therefore, is a cosmic consciousness of a transpersonal, trans-social and transplanetary nature, that integrates these three aspects into a broader perspective.

Just as peace can be viewed from a fragmentary perspective or a holistic one, so has education, too, been fragmented and distorted. The time has come for a new approach; one that takes into account the fact that it is desirable for studying, learning and peace management to be the fruit of interdisciplinary and transdisciplinary work.

It is this that we are going to look at now, beginning with a sum-mary of the effects of the established paradigm on education.

Table 2. Visions of peace according to the old and new paradigms

Established paradigm	Holistic paradigm
Peace seen as an external phenomenon	*Peace seen as an external and internal phenomenon*
On the external level	
• As the absence of conflict and violence. Many theories, cultural, judicial, socio-economic, military, religious. • As a state of harmony and brotherhood between people and with nature.	Peace is the result of a convergence of measures relating to inner ecology, social ecology, in which the principal theories of the established paradigm are taken into consideration and find their place in an integrated manner.
On the inner level	
• Peace is seen as the absence or result of dissolution of intra-psychological conflicts. • As a state of inner harmony.	This convergence results in a transpersonal state of consciousness, of which peace is one of the manifestations.
There is a lack of integration of these various points of view.	

Chapter 2

Education

The fragmented view of education

What is called 'education' today is very often confused with teaching. Teaching is aimed only at a person's intellectual or sensory capabilities. It is no more than a mental communication that adds to our amount of knowledge or influences our opinions.

This kind of teaching has become the exclusive domain of schools, while it is assumed that the family takes responsibility for character development, which includes feelings, emotions, habits and inner attitudes.

In fact, everything indicates that families are increasingly copying schools; the excessive breadth of curriculum is to a large extent disrupting the relationship between parents and children. The family is progressively becoming an extension of school.

This has led to a schism between thought and action, between on the one hand opinions and attitudes fostered to a large extent by school, and on the other hand the habits and behaviour instilled by the family.

We would like to mention at this point the results of surveys of racial attitudes in certain countries. If we consult public opinion, a large majority of Whites say that they oppose racism. This is almost certainly something they learned at school. But if they are asked whether they would allow their daughter to marry a Black man, the response of that same majority is negative. This answer must arise from the traditions and habits of the family. Other examples abound: it is possible to have democratic opinions and behave tyrannically; to defend the environment and step on flowers and ants; to declare yourself non-violent and hit your children; to claim to be tolerant and gossip behind everybody's back; to have democratic opinions and behave autocratically; to defend ecology and use polluting household products at home; or buy over-packaged products or disposable plastic plates for a party.

Confusing teaching with education brings about another fragmentation to the extent that knowledge is continuously broken down into further specialities and sub-specialities, as is the case in secondary teaching, and even more so in higher education.

The holistic approach in education provides us with a very different vision and set of methods that are part of a transdisciplinary approach. This is what we shall look at now.

The holistic view of education

When education is confused with teaching, the accent is placed on the mind. A holistic approach aims to awaken and develop the intuition as much as the mind and the feelings as much as the senses. The goal is to achieve a balance between these psychic functions. As far as the brain is concerned, this would correspond to a balance between its right and left hemispheres and to a circulation of energy between the cortical and sub-cortical layers, as well as throughout the whole cerebral-spinal system.

Whereas teaching emphasizes the contents of a course and the acquisition of facts, the holistic approach shows us how every situation in life offers us the opportunity to learn; moreover, there is an emphasis on developing the ability to teach ourselves. The global and specific contexts of every situation take on an equal importance.

Traditional education has a tendency to condition people to live exclusively in the outer world, while the holistic approach orients them towards the inner world as well as the outer.

We could also make a comparison between the orientation of the contents of traditional education and those of holistic education. The first approach emphasizes consumption, aggressive competition, success, excessive specialization, acquisition and material affluence. The holistic approach demands voluntary simplicity, co-operation, human values, general knowledge prior to specialized knowledge, and sees money as something to be used to serve fundamental values rather than as an end in itself.

In addition to all these differences, there is a basic one that lies in the concept of human evolution and our capacity for transformation. The established paradigm is in the grip of a static perspective in the sense that there is a general belief that our intellectual and emotional development ceases after adolescence.

From the holistic point of view, evolution continues after adolescence. In fact it acknowledges that we can go through a complete metamorphosis, like that of caterpillar to butterfly. Metaphorically speaking, the caterpillar symbolizes the human being tied into a web of habits, prejudices and daily routines. The chrysalis represents the process of transformation from a consciousness of egoism, withdrawal, limitation and fear, to one of breadth, harmony and altruism, it involves a period of inner crisis, a questioning of previous values, a temporary dark night of the soul. The butterfly would be the new state of consciousness characterized by a state of peace and fulfilment.

A few words here about educational methodology. According to the traditional mechanistic paradigm, the student is seen as a piece of magnetic tape or a blank film on to which the teacher mechanically transfers the lesson. The student is expected to make an effort to memorize things in order to reinforce the teacher's work. The process is expected to bring about the changes recommended in the lesson. Instead of being the object of teaching, the new paradigm replaces the concept of passive students with that of students who actively participate in the process, who take their transformation into their own hands and chart their own course (see Table 3).

It is in this direction that since the beginning of the twentieth century we have been witnessing a very slow evolution in educational methods. 'Active' education is gradually replacing 'passive' education. The slowness of its adoption is due to centuries of deeply rooted habits which delay the assumption of new attitudes.

In this new or active kind of education it is up to the student to work, to undertake research, to visit places, to make observations on the ground, to create personal written or oral reports. In this latter case it is the student who gives the lesson, the teacher becomes the expert, the consultant; he/she gives pointers rather than teaches, provides an example by his/her behaviour, showing that the principles he/she advocates are deeply rooted in his/her daily life.

The scope of this work does not allow us here to expand on the subject of active education. There are numerous studies on this topic and various methods of applying it, and it has proved to be more effective in encouraging the evolution of the person as a whole than have traditional teaching techniques.

Before concluding this chapter I would like to draw your attention to the fact that both the shift in paradigm and the change in educational methods are a specific phenomenon of the industrialized societies as well as those that have been influenced by the Western world. It

Table 3. The old and the new paradigm in education

	ESTABLISHED PARADIGM	HOLISTIC PARADIGM
CONCEPT OF EDUCATION	Information. Teaching limited to the intellect. Instruction aimed at memory and reason.	Training. Education of the whole person. Process of harmonization and full development of senses, feelings, reason and intuition.
CONCEPT OF STUDENT	The pupil considered as an 'object', as an automatic mechanism of recording.	The pupil considered as a 'subject', as an active participant in the educative process.
NERVOUS SYSTEM	Left side of brain.	Left and right sides of brain. The whole cerebro-spinal system.
FIELD OF ACTION	Acquisition of knowledge; accent on content. Changing of opinions.	Transformation of the personality in its entirety. Changing of opinions, attitudes and behaviours.
EDUCATIVE AGENT	School as an agent of intellectual education, with the family as an auxiliary of school. The 'educator' as 'teacher'.	Family, school and society in a joint effort. The educator as animator, facilitator, focalizer and even catalyst of evolution.
CONCEPT OF EVOLUTION	Evolution ceases at adolescence. Maturity limited to the intellect, to the capacity to procreate and to work. This evolution is personal.	Evolution continues with adulthood. Maturity seen as a state of broadened consciousness, of harmony, fulfilment and peace of a personal and transpersonal nature.
TYPE OF TRAINING	Predominance of specialization.	General training takes precedence over specialization.
ORIENTATION OF VALUES	Pragmatic values: consumption, competition, power, possessiveness, celebrity.	Pragmatic and ethical values: voluntary simplicity, co-operation, generosity, sharing, equality, equanimity.
METHODS OF EDUCATION	Verbal explanation, spoken, complemented by books and textbooks. Passive method. Rewards and punishments in a selective system. The teacher teaches, the pupil listens. School separate from the community. The teacher 'recommends' opinions, attitudes and changes of behaviour.	Research and individual and group study. Spoken verbal presentations by students and teacher. Active method. Audiovisual methods. Presentations, excursions, visits. Student is active, does research and teaches others. The teacher as advisor, consultant, guide. School integrated into the community. Educator is a living example of the principles and behaviour he/she recommends.

seems that societies that live in harmony with nature, and are more closely integrated into their environment, use methods of education that are rooted in action and that count on the participation of the whole community.

Now that we have defined peace and education in relation to the paradigm shift, we can go on to discuss the nature of education for peace.

Chapter 3

Towards a holistic view of education for peace

As we have seen, the traditional Newtonian-Cartesian paradigm has brought us – both despite and partly as a consequence of the enormous benefits and luxuries it provides – to the verge of destroying the planet and to violent solutions to conflicts.

This paradigm also provides us with a muddled and fragmented vision of peace and a reductionist view of education, with confusion between real education and mere intellectual instruction.

According to the holistic paradigm, education for peace is based on a new vision of education and a new sense of peace, as described above.

We could define holistic education for peace as follows: holistic education for peace is a method of education inspired by active methods, directed to the person as a whole to help him or her maintain or re-establish harmony between senses, feelings, mind and intuition. It is concerned with physical health, along with emotional and mental equilibrium, and the awakening and sustenance of human values. 'Everything which exists is part of an interdependent universe. All living beings depend on one another for their existence, well-being and development.'[1]

At the social level, holistic education for peace addresses the task of developing the skills with which to manage conflicts in a non-violent manner and to transform destructive forms of energy into constructive action on the cultural, social, political and economic levels.

---

1. *Declaration of Human Responsibilities for Peace and Sustainable Development*, Article 1, University of Peace, Costa Rica, 1989.

As far as the relationship between humans and the environment is concerned, the aim of holistic education is to teach people to repair, to whatever extent possible, the ecological destruction caused by humans and to maintain the balance of the ecosystem.

Basically, then, it is about instilling an 'art of living in peace'. This art must be developed at three levels:

- Human: inner ecology or the art of living in peace with oneself.
- Social: social ecology or the art of living in peace with others.
- Environmental: planetary ecology or the art of living in peace with nature.

At the human level this education will awaken simultaneously or in succession:

- Peace of the body.
- Peace of the heart.[2]
- Peace of the mind.

At the social level the art of living in peace is addressed to three different areas:

- The economy.
- Social and political life.
- Culture.

At the environmental level holistic education will look for the best solutions for living in peace with the environment, while taking into consideration the three different forms of energy:

- Matter (solid, liquid, fire, gas).
- Life (vegetable, animal and human).
- Information (atomic, genetic, cerebral).

Doing this will broaden the field of consciousness in three areas:

- Personal egocentric consciousness.
- Social anthropocentric consciousness.
- Planetary geocentric consciousness.

In going beyond these three forms of awareness, the art of living in peace opens doors to the holistic vision characterized by a transpersonal state of cosmic consciousness.

This, then, is a general outline of holistic education for peace as taught by 'the art of living in peace'. Before concluding Part Two, a few words about a basic methodological principle follow: holistic education

2.   A UNESCO study recommends a 'socioaffective' approach, based on experience. See *Education for International Co-operation and Peace at the Primary School Level,* Paris, UNESCO, 1985.

for peace cannot be limited to the classroom; it is an apprenticeship in which self-training must be encouraged.

The work we present here is an attempt to develop a self-training programme, in the sense discussed by Abraham Moles in a UNESCO publication,[3] where he introduces the concept of 'self-learning'. It is an invitation, even though part of a course, to explore and verify through personal experience the foundations of thousands of years of traditional wisdom, checked and verified to some degree by modern science, in the spirit of UNESCO's Venice Declaration.

What we are proposing here is a system in which, to quote Abraham Moles, education would tend 'once again to merge with the uncertainties of daily life; it would regain some of the characteristics of direct apprenticeship which the tribe or old-style village offered to its young people outside school'.[4]

Methods of education

In the short, medium and long terms the reading of this general introduction can be enriched by the following activities:

* Discussion groups on the various themes.
* Visiting educational institutions which practise these active methods of education.
* Group study and discussion of the paradigm shift.

We recommend the following authors:

BOHM, D. *The Undivided Universe*. London, Routledge.

CAPRA, F. *The Turning Point*. Bantam/Flamingo, 1983.

FERGUSON, M. *The Aquarian Conspiracy*. Torcher/Paladin, 1982.

KUHN, T. *The Structure of Scientific Revolutions*. University of Chicago Press, 1970.

NICOLESCU, B. *Nous, la Particule et le Monde*. Paris, Le Mail, 1985.

WEIL, P. *L'Homme Sans Frontières*. Paris, L'Espace Bleu, 1989.

_____. P. Vers une Approche Holistique de la Nature de la Réalité. *Question No. 64*. Paris, Albin Michel, 1986.

3.   A. Moles, *Media Education*, Paris, UNESCO, 1985.
4.   Ibid.

Training others
in the art of living in peace

For peace educators to be able to pass on the 'art of living in peace' to other people, whether children, youth or adults, they must fulfil an essential preliminary condition: they themselves must be an example of what they teach. One could say that their very being, by radiating qualities such as affection, gentleness, patience, openness to the needs of others, the ability to put themselves in somebody else's shoes, and so on, would render all other forms of instruction unnecessary.

The essential question, then, is to know how to find such educators or, if they are few and far between (which seems to be the case), how to prepare and train them.

In the first case, it is a matter of choice: of recruitment and of selection. In the second case, it is a matter of training.

In fact the qualities necessary in a peace educator are very similar to those of outstanding individuals, the great masters, examples of whom exist in all cultures – men and women who have integrated wisdom and love into their everyday existence and who have dedicated their lives to the service of these values.

These people, even though they exist in our day, are rare. A Gandhi, or a Mother Teresa, is not born every day.

What we can do is to find people who identify with the masters or with these qualities, who work on themselves and who have sufficient clarity and modesty to show themselves as they really are, while in the first place behaving in harmony with the great human values such as truth, beauty and altruistic love. Some such people exist and fortunately all indications are that they are gradually growing in number as the threat of extinction of life on the planet increases.

To give these people additional training that will allow them to pass on the 'art of living in peace', while concurrently training themselves with the methods outlined in this book, is the sensible solution that we have devised.

To this end, it is necessary that future educators in the 'art of living in peace' undergo the same learning process, for the reasons stated above. We shall begin with a description of the process of the destruction of peace.

In this book we are going to present a fundamental theory of the process in the form of brief statements. Each constitutes a short synthesis of theoretical points of view or research results, in the various scientific fields and/or traditional wisdom.

Each statement may be developed according to the students' interests and the time available to apply the whole programme. They are summed up in the form of tables that can be presented using a floppy disk, projected on to a screen or written on a blackboard for group discussion.

To serve our purpose, we have systematically developed a dual approach that consists in analysing the peace destruction process followed by an exploration of the transformation process that allows peace to be restored.

In other words, as the first step is to identify the deep causes of the sickness in order to better identify the remedy, we are now going to begin by describing the peace destruction process.

Chapter 1

The art of living in peace with oneself

The destruction of peace process

In order to know how to awaken and 'rebuild' peace, nothing is more necessary than an in-depth understanding of the process that has led the human race to risk destroying life on the planet.

How was war born in the human mind?

As the preamble to UNESCO's Constitution says so well, it is effectively in our mind – in other words, at the level of our thoughts and emotions – that the seeds of violence and war are born. They later take root in our physical body, particularly in our muscles. Nevertheless, this statement is not enough. It runs the risk of becoming dogma if we do not attempt to demonstrate the process in an experimental or experiential fashion. Simply examining our own experience confirms this preamble.

In fact we have already given above a general outline of the phenomenon of the seeding of violence, when we described how the general process of the destruction of peace takes place.

To understand this process better at the human level, we must go deeper and describe in detail how this destruction happens within ourselves. This description will be accompanied by real-life experiences in line with the recommendations that follow this explanation. These experiences provide an opportunity to escape from the intellectual and explanatory level on which we are meeting now, in reading the intellectual part of this module, and to confirm in real life – literally, in the flesh – the authenticity of these statements.

It is a vicious circle of compulsive repetition, in which almost all of humanity finds itself caught, a kind of optical illusion.

Figure. 1. The wheel of destruction

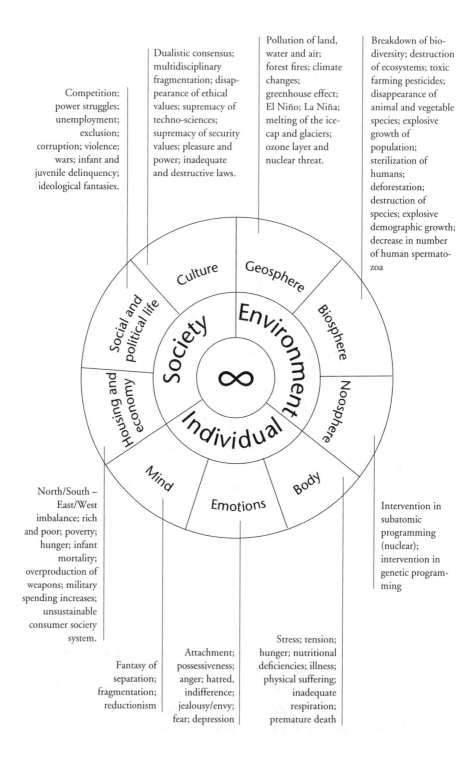

Dualistic consensus; multidisciplinary fragmentation; disappearance of ethical values; supremacy of techno-sciences; supremacy of security values; pleasure and power; inadequate and destructive laws.

Pollution of land, water and air; forest fires; climate changes; greenhouse effect; El Niño; La Niña; melting of the ice-cap and glaciers; ozone layer and nuclear threat.

Competition; power struggles; unemployment; exclusion; corruption; violence; wars; infant and juvenile delinquency; ideological fantasies.

Breakdown of bio-diversity; destruction of ecosystems; toxic farming pesticides; disappearance of animal and vegetable species; explosive growth of population; sterilization of humans; deforestation; destruction of species; explosive demographic growth; decrease in number of human spermatozoa

North/South – East/West imbalance; rich and poor; poverty; hunger; infant mortality; overproduction of weapons; military spending increases; unsustainable consumer society system.

Intervention in subatomic programming (nuclear); intervention in genetic programming

Fantasy of separation; fragmentation; reductionism

Attachment; possessiveness; anger; hatred, indifference; jealousy/envy; fear; depression

Stress; tension; hunger; nutritional deficiencies; illness; physical suffering; inadequate respiration; premature death

This process takes place almost simultaneously on three basic levels which correspond, as we have already seen, to the three basic forms of energy:

- The physical level of our body.
- The emotional level of our life.
- The mental level of our thoughts and concepts (see overleaf).

The fantasy of separation and crisis of fragmentation

At the mental level an illusion takes shape which we call the fantasy of separation. It is a permanent phenomenon of our mental world. It consists of the belief that we are separate from the outside world, that the 'I' and the universe do not have any connection with each other. It is possible to create an experience of this in a very simple way. Point with your finger to where nature is and where the universe is. Our immediate reaction is to point our finger outside ourselves, at trees, at the garden or at anything outside our own bodies. It is at that moment that the separation of subject and object takes place.

This separation has a long history and starts very early. Some people believe it begins when the baby sees his mother's breast, or at birth, or even before that. In fact, this separation is only an appearance, it has the practical function of bringing us into existence but in reality it is illusory.

If, for example, we examine under an electron microscope the human body, the air or any object, we cannot avoid concluding, as is shown by quantum physics, that there is nothing there except space-energy. At the final count, when someone looks at something, it is as if space is looking at space across space. All indications are that this space is a void that is not empty. It is full of the potential of everything that exists. From the moment when we begin to regard the outside world as separate, we start to create limits in our minds, imaginary frontiers. All conflicts are born on these frontiers. In fact space does not have any frontiers – it is all one, a continuum.

Another direct consequence of this fantasy of separation is that the subject, believing in his own solidity and that of the external world, becomes attached to everything that is pleasurable, rejects everything that is likely to cause him displeasure or suffering, and remains indifferent to all else.

Fundamental theory of the process
of the destruction of peace

The Venice Declaration recommends the reconciliation of the sciences and the spiritual traditions. This coming together leads to an ultimate conception of reality: an infinite and atemporal primordial space.

◆

From this space emanates the energy of all the known systems.

◆

All the known systems of the universe are energy systems, 'composed' of the same energy.

◆

This energy takes three indivisible forms:
– Informational (intelligence).
– Biological (life).
– Physical (matter).

◆

This, then, is a non-fragmentary theory of energy.

◆

Human beings are an integral part of this energy system.

◆

They also are made of the following, all of which are inseparable from the whole:
– Matter (body).
– Life (emotions).
– Information (mind).

◆

But by means of thought human beings separate themselves from the universe. They create a fantasy of separation:
– Subject – object.
– Me – the world.
– Humans – the universe.

◆

The human mind creates boundaries in space. But space does not have any limits.

◆

By their thoughts human beings separate themselves from society and from nature. In their mind they forget that Nature, Society and Humankind are inseparable. Moreover, mind is separated from the information of the whole. Human mind is separated from the universal mind.

Within the individual, mind separates itself from the emotions (life) and from the body (matter).

◆

So a process of destruction of the personal ecology begins. A fragmentation affects the human being. In his mind the fantasy of separation engenders a paradigm of separation.

◆

Because he feels fragmented, he generates destructive emotions on the level of life, specifically attachment and possessiveness of people, things and ideas which give him pleasure. These destructive emotions generate stress, which destroys the equilibrium of the body.

◆

Because people believe they are separate from society, they create a piecemeal culture, a violent social life and exploitative economic conditions.

◆

The individual projects his or her fragmentation on the level of knowledge.

◆

These social conditions reinforce in their turn the suffering of the individual.

◆

A society which exploits human beings increases separation and grows into an unbridled exploitation of nature. It intervenes in information, in the nuclear industry and genetic manipulation. It destroys the ecosystems and threatens life on the planet. Lastly, it destroys and pollutes the elements of matter.

◆

And this is how the self-reinforcing vicious circle of self-destruction of humankind and of planetary life functions.

◆

The function of holistic education for peace is to transform these obstacles into positive forms of energy (see Figure 2).

In fact, everything indicates that we are made for pleasure, joy and happiness. We spend our lives in search of these things. Except we only look for them outside ourselves. We could call it the neurosis of paradise lost. The lost paradise exists within ourselves. Peace is part of this lost paradise. It is a mood or state of consciousness. The problem is not pleasure in itself, but our attachment to the object that gives us pleasure. After the establishment of the fantasy of separation we became attached to objects, people or ideas.

The emotional reaction that generally follows the attachment is fear: fear of losing or being robbed of the object which we think we possess. Whether it is a jewel, a lover or a good idea, the pattern is the same.

Fear of loss gives rise to destructive emotions like distrust, jealousy, aggression, wounded pride and depression.

These emotions are responsible for and constitute stress; they form a whole which can be called mental suffering. But stress also causes us to experience physical pain through sickness.

Mental suffering and physical pain in their turn strengthen and reinforce the fantasy of separation.

This is how the personal vicious circle of compulsive repetition is formed, which leads to the loss of our inner, interpersonal and social peace (see Figure 2).

Figure 2. The wheel of peace
The transformation process

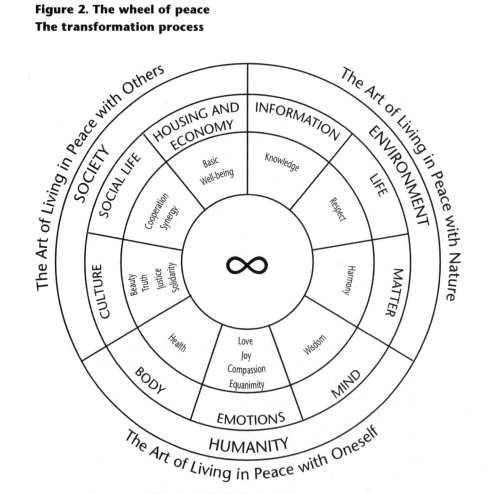

Figure 3. The fantasy of separation

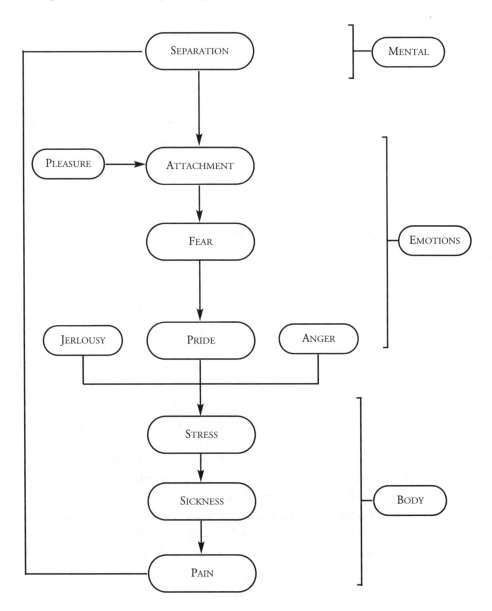

Methods of education

As we have mentioned before, during this phase it is important that the student, or better still the 'trainee', observes by him/herself and within him/herself the truth of these statements. He/she has to discover to what extent he/she is a victim of the vicious circle of compulsive repetition and to what extent he/she is controlled by the neurosis of paradise lost.

Short-term programme

- Start with a theoretical explanation, accompanied by a diagram (Figure 2).
- In order to demonstrate the fantasy of separation, ask your students to point to nature.
- Invite the group to role-play on the following theme: A young man and woman meet for the first time; it is love at first sight; they set up a date in a cafe; this meeting is interrupted by the young man's lover; a scene of anger and jealousy; the young woman falls ill; her mother calls the doctor.
- Group discussion with the help of Figure 3.

Medium- and long-term programme

- Use the above short-term programme as an introduction.
- Continue with a long course and study of the fundamental theory of the destruction of peace; historical research on the process of fragmentation and destruction of peace.
- Make a wall newspaper, where the 'trainees' periodically stick cuttings from magazines and newspapers illustrating the consequences of attachment and possessiveness in individual and collective life.
- Organize a series of discussions where students use personal case histories illustrating the vicious circle of compulsive repetition.
- Invite an expert in group dynamics or encounter groups to help the group discover its own inner obstacles to peace.
- Analyse a historical conflict that took place in your country, applying the contents of Table 4.

The first phase provokes a strong motivation in a large number of trainees to discover a means of breaking out of the vicious circle. The group is then ready to embark on the rest of the programme: the awakening and development of inner peace.

The awakening and development of inner peace

As we have seen, it is possible to distinguish various seats of inner peace: peace of the body, peace of the heart and peace of mind. This phase exists mainly to allow trainees to locate within themselves and get in touch with the different kinds of inner peace.

These are so interdependent that it is difficult to distinguish between them; if we do so, it is only as an aid to understanding them;

Table 4. The causes of war and peace

FIELDS	CAUSES OF WAR	CAUSES OF PEACE
SCIENCE	Concept of total objectivity	Concept of subjectivity
PSYCHOLOGY	Concept of separation Hatred Ignorance	Concept of inter- dependence and unity Love Knowledge
MILITARY	Fear 'Whoever wants peace prepare for War'	Trust 'Whoever wants peace prepare for peace'
LEGAL	Concept of a just war Right to use force National sovereignty	Unjust war (Each human being's right to peace). The force of what is right National interdependence
ECONOMIC	Hunger and poverty Competition	Basic comfort Co-operation
SOCIAL AND POLITICAL	Ideological conflicts	Ideological exchanges
RELIGION	Religious wars	Inter-faith encounters

otherwise it would mean reverting to the kind of fragmentation that we are trying to leave behind.

Therefore peace of the body also involves the other two aspects of inner peace.

Peace of the body

Our body is a physical system of dense energy, of matter through which vital and psychic energy circulates. This energy is given different names depending on the cultural milieu. In yoga it is called *prana*, in Tibet *rlung*, in Greece *pneuma*, in Hebrew *ruach*, in China it is known as *ki*, in Polynesia as *mana*, among the Dakota as *wakanda*, and in ancient Egypt it was called *ka*.

According to these traditions, this energy circulates through subtle channels that are well known in Chinese acupuncture and in Chinese and Japanese micromassage. Free circulation of this energy and its balanced distribution throughout the body would correspond to a state of harmony and peace. Destructive emotions, as described above, create among other effects blockages in the form of more or less chronic knots of muscular tension depending on the occurrence of emotional crises during the course of life.

We find similar concepts in psychotherapy and psychology. Different schools give energy different names: libido (Freud, Jung), *orgone* (Reich), *élan vital* (Bergson), psychotronic energy (Krippner). Unblocking these knots of tension, relaxing what Reich called character armour, is what both traditional methods and modern bioenergetic methods are trying to achieve. From the moment one is able to undo these knots of tension, one's energy once again becomes available and starts to circulate again throughout one's whole body.

The main effect of this is a state of peace, of tranquillity, which fosters a broader state of consciousness and a harmonious psycho-somatic condition.

Some of the methods for achieving this are: relaxation as prac-tised in sophrology and yoga, particularly hatha yoga; Tai Chi Chuan, which is like a slow dance; and the martial arts like Japanese judo and aikido.

Yoga relaxation has inspired research in the field of psycho-somatic medicine. Due particularly to the 'autogenic training' of Schultz[1] and Caycedo's sophrology,[2] there is no longer any doubt that this approach provides a physical base for peace of the emotions and the mind. Psychophysical measurements have amply confirmed what we all experience in our own lives.

A programme aimed at personal experience and at achieving this first kind of peace, has to begin with some form of relaxation.

Relaxation provides the following advantages:

- It enables us to create a somatic basis for inner peace.
- It allows us to go through the day in a calm state, if it is practised every morning.
- It helps to keep us healthy.
- It aids medical treatment in the healing of a large number of psychosomatic illnesses.
- It helps to alleviate or even quickly eliminate a nervous or tense state.
- It cures insomnia.
- It does away with sleepiness during the day.

1.   J. H. Schulz, *Le Training Autogène*, Paris, PUF, 1965.
2.   A. Caycedo, *L'Avenir de la Sophrologie*, Paris, Retz, 1979.

- It facilitates creativity.
- It leads us into other states of consciousness.
- It is a preparation for meditation as we shall see later.

A healthy and balanced diet reinforces the peace of the body. Yoga, for example, teaches us that there are three kinds of food: heavy foods which encourage torpor and passivity, energizing foods which stir us up and push us to physical activity, and those foods which facilitate harmony and inner peace. Yoga recommends a natural and vegetarian diet. It is interesting to note that a reduction in human consumption of meat would free up agricultural land for sufficient food production to eliminate hunger in the developing countries.[3]

Peace of the heart

As stated previously, the emotional and affective aspects of peace are too often neglected in research and education for peace, due to a predominantly intellectual approach. Yet it is evident to all who are concerned with feelings and emotions that they play as fundamental a role in inner and even social peace as they do in violence and war.

What is inner peace if not a state of harmony and fulfilment, where feelings of joy and love can find free expression? What can we pass on to our 'trainees' in peace? How to create peace at a feeling level?

This is a very important question and various answers have been given. Each one recommends a method for attaining peace. Some are very simple and can be practised by anyone. Others require the guidance of a master or a therapist, depending on the culture in which one lives.

We shall attempt to give here a very short description of these methods. A great deal of study and comparative research on the results obtained is necessary in the field of experimental education in order to determine which techniques are the most effective. But there is to some extent a consensus that the ability of the educator to give of himself with devotion and love is as important, or even more so, than the actual method itself. One can also imagine that the motivation and devotion of the 'trainee' is essential for the ongoing practice of each technique.

It is possible to distinguish two major categories of methods: those which take as their point of departure the destructive emotions like hate and anger, and those which tend to awaken and develop the positive emotions that lead to peace. These latter are inseparable from

3.   UNEP, *Personal Action Guide for the Earth*, Santa Monica, United Nations Environment Programme.

peace of the mind and even that of the body, and we deal with them later.

Methods of energy transformation

We shall now discuss the methods which deal with destructive emotions with a view to transforming or dissolving them – without, however, suppressing them.

Direct awareness

This is the simplest method. It consists of recognizing the destructive emotion at the moment when it appears. According to the yoga tradition, and in particular the Tibetan one, there are five factors or 'poisons' that destroy peace, of which four are of a purely emotional nature and the fifth is cognitive.

This last one refers to the fantasy of separation and is called ignorance or misconception.

The other four, which are related to one another, are attachment, anger, jealousy and pride. It is at the moment when these emotions come into being that we can become aware of them. To start with, this direct awareness of the emotion's origin comes too late – for example, anger may have already produced its effects. All we can do at this stage is to recognize that we have been taken over by the emotion. Gradually we become aware when it is happening and eventually we are able to see it coming. This last is the ideal condition. Experience suggests that when we are able to do this, our anger dissolves and its energy transforms into positive feelings.

Gandhi's *ahimsa* method of non-violence

Advocated by Gandhi, *ahimsa* means far more than non-violence. It is about transforming feelings of hate into feelings of love. The success of Gandhi in bringing about the independence of India through nationwide non-violent action constitutes a very impressive demonstration of the power of *ahimsa*. Used in a number of countries today, it requires total self-awareness and constant attention to what is going on within oneself.[4]

4.   L. del Vasto, *Technique de la Non Violence*, Paris, Denoel-Gonthier, 1971.

Psychotherapeutic methods

For many people the above methods fail because of deeply rooted negative habits and ingrained parental and cultural models, and more particularly because of identification with educators who are themselves
violent. Often a child's violent reactions cannot be expressed and they
remain blocked in the body and the mind until adulthood; they still
want to be expressed and they eventually burst out in an inadequate and
compulsive manner.

In this book we shall confine ourselves to talking about only
some of the therapeutic techniques which aim at unblocking and free-
ing violence and the seeds of aggression. Today hundreds of psychotherapeutic methods exist, among which are: Freudian psychoanalysis,
Jungian analysis, Moreno's psychodrama, Fritz Perls' gestalt therapy,
Wilhelm Reich's orgone therapy, Lowen's bioenergetics, Desoille's day-
dream therapy, Assagioli's psychosynthesis, Carl Rogers' person-centred
therapy and Victor Frankl's logotherapy.

The peace educator cannot absorb all these techniques, nor
apply them, for that is something that requires long training. He/she
can, however, undertake one of them, which seems to fulfil his/her own
personal needs. This helps one to recognize the needs of one's own
'trainees' and to guide them, as necessary, towards a particular therapy
or therapist.

Methods for awakening peace

Instead of trying to transform a heart of conflict into a heart of peace, it
is possible to awaken peace directly.

'Responsibility is an inherent aspect of any relation in which
human beings are involved. This capacity to act responsibly in a conscious, independent, unique and personal manner is an inalienable
creative quality of every human being. There is no limit to its scope or
depth other than that established by each person for himself. The more
it is acted upon and put into practice, the more it will grow and become
strengthened.'[5]

In each one of us slumber the functions or qualities of the heart
that are directly responsible for maintaining inner and social peace. The

5. *Declaration of Human Responsibilities for Lasting Peace and Sustainable Development.*
Article 6, Chapter III, Costa Rica, United Nations University of Peace, 1989.

spiritual traditions are unanimous on this point. We can summarize these qualities as follows:

- *Joy.* As we have already mentioned, we are made for a life of joy, especially the kind we experience when we see the joy of others.
- *Altruistic love.* This can be defined as a feeling of wanting everybody's happiness and acting accordingly.
- *Compassion.* How can we live in peace knowing that suffering and poverty exist all around us? Compassion is precisely the feeling of wanting to heal these ills and of moving heaven and earth to achieve it.

The universality of the above three feelings is very important; they apply to every living species without bias. If they were really put into practice by everybody towards everybody else, would there still be wars and conflicts?

These qualities can be awakened and developed in different ways. In the first place this can be achieved by the example of the educator who interiorizes them and integrates them into his daily life. One cannot emphasize this point enough. We can also call on methods of visualization such as are employed in day-dream therapy and, more specifically, in psychosynthesis. This involves asking students, when they are in a relaxed state, to imagine from time to time an actual scene from their daily lives where these qualities are put into practice. It is a mind-programming which facilitates the following method. This consists of informing the student about these qualities by defining them, as we have done here, and encouraging their application in daily life, showing the student that this path leads to peace.

Since the methods for awakening peace of the heart are inseparable from those for awakening peace of mind, we shall now proceed to concentrate on these.

Peace of mind

First let us turn our attention to the term 'mind'. In French *esprit* (mind) has two different meanings:

- It corresponds to the English word 'mind' and can be understood as 'mental'. It refers to the collection of mental faculties we possess such as intelligence, perception, memory and so on.
- It also refers to a form of subtle energy, called 'spiritual energy' by Bergson, to a principle of life, consciousness and thought, as opposed to the body, which is made of matter. In this sense it is linked to moral or so-called 'higher' values.

The holistic view goes beyond any kind of opposites or dualities, embracing and integrating them. Thanks to the non-fragmentary theory of energy, in which the lines of expression assume three forms of an opposing and independent appearance – matter (body), life (movement and emotions) and information (psyche) – but are in fact linked in a continuous evolutionary chain, the duality of matter and mind tends to dissolve.

That is why we are adopting a wider approach of spirituality and the mind. This term indicates a stage at which everything is beyond the mind and the psyche and which integrates and comprises them.[6] In this sense the human being would be an energy transformer, the same energy, whether manifested as matter, life or mind. What we call mind is nothing other, perhaps, than energy itself in its primordial state and which through human beings returns to that state.

Everything indicates that total peace is achieved in this transpersonal state, which is studied by transpersonal psychology and which is found at the basis of all the great spiritual traditions.[7]

So, by the term 'mind' we imply this whole collection of energies – psyche, mind and spirituality – distinguishing between them to facilitate the teaching process.

Let us take a look at the techniques which help us attain peace of mind. Because of the holistic approach we are taking, these methods include peace of the body, peace of the heart and peace of mind.

Even relaxation, which we have introduced as a tool to create peace of the body, has emotional and mental repercussions. It spreads physical peace into the heart and mind.

The most important objective is to get to the point where we can go beyond and dissolve the fantasy of separation. We can achieve this by going beyond thought, the nature of which is to fragment, classify, divide. Thought, intelligence and reason are precious dialectical tools indispensable for daily life and our mental evolution. But at the same time thought is the big obstacle to evolution towards a holistic vision.

The best method for helping us to go beyond thought, while honouring its gifts, is meditation.

Meditation

Meditation has been defined in several ways. In fact this is a paradox since it is a method that consists of sitting down and doing nothing. It is

6.   Th. Brosse, *La Conscience Energie*, Paris, Presence, 1979.
7.   P. Weil, *Anthologie de l'Extase*, Paris, Question de . . . Albin Michel, 1989; S. Grof, *Transpersonal Psychology* (audio cassette from *Sounds True*).

a return to oneself, to one's own body. In other words, it is about doing the opposite to what our industrial civilization has conditioned us to do: to live outside ourselves, to direct all our activity towards the outside world, at the risk of reinforcing the fantasy of separation.

This apparent non-activity is coupled with attention, observation and a mind open to everything that happens. The person who is meditating concentrates on a thought, an inner image, a sound or an object such as the flame of a candle. It does not matter what the object of concentration is; the important thing is the result – rambling thoughts die down and with them the ideas that separate the self from external objects, as well as separating the external objects themselves.

'All human beings are an inseparable part of nature, upon which culture and human civilization have been built.'

'Life on Earth is abundant and diverse. It is sustained by the unhindered functioning of natural systems that ensure the provision of energy, air, water and nutrients for all living creatures. Every manifestation of life on Earth is unique and essential and must therefore be respected and protected without regard to its apparent value to human beings.'[8]

When we reach this state, the frontier between the 'I' and the external world dissolves and, among other effects, inner peace is regained.

Much criticism has been directed against this technique by people who are misinformed, misguided or have only read about meditation. The main criticism is that meditation alienates us from the material world at the heart of industrial civilization. In fact the reverse is true. Research done on the subject shows that meditation contributes directly to the improvement of the following functions: mental state, attention, memory, emotional equilibrium, synchronization of the brainwaves of the two hemispheres of the brain, and productivity at work. Because it awakens our consciousness, meditation is the antidote to alienation.

To go within ourselves for twenty minutes each morning and evening does not mean that we are isolating ourselves from the outside world, but rather that we are learning to become more open, more conscious and less of an automaton – in other words, less alienated.

Above all, returning to our main topic, meditation helps to address the usual issues of daily life in a harmonious and peaceful

8. *Declaration of Human Responsibilities for Peace and Sustainable Development*, Articles 2 and 3, Chapter 1, Costa Rica, United Nations University of Peace, 1989.

way. Conflicts continue but they are resolved without violence, with friendship and wisdom. A spirit of serenity takes over the conflict and allows us to find a solution within ourselves and with others.

All that we have said about meditation also applies to dance in its meditative forms, such as tai chi. Originating from Taoism, this is still a national custom in China, and is practised by millions of Chinese in public places. Its essentials have been extracted to make it accessible to the West.

In Africa, Asia, Latin America and the Middle East, numerous ritual dances, through conscious trance, achieve similar effects – although research on an intercultural basis would be necessary to prove or disprove this last point.

In conclusion, meditative practices lead to what Abraham Maslow has called peak states or experiences, capable of unblocking and awakening the higher human and spiritual values, the same ones used by Gorbachev to motivate the Soviet worker.[9]

Table 5 gives a summary of these values classified according to the human centres of energy (*chakras*), as described by yoga. Each of these centres, of which there are seven principal ones, corresponds to a different school of philosophy and psychology, all of which apparently contradict one another.[10] The centres can be used as an exclusive basis for the explanation and conciliation of opposing ideologies. This system could be an important instrument of peace, if detailed research were devoted to it.

Dualistic in appearance, our classification of values into constructive and destructive behaviours does not in any way imply that we view them in an absolute fashion. For example, we build a new building from the destruction of the old. The evolution of all that exists implies a continuous transformation of opposites into each other.

We can say the same thing about the hierarchy of values: it is only an appearance of experiences of different qualities at the level of existence. In fact, it is the manifestation in the human being of the same energy.

These concepts and techniques that enable us to awaken and develop the art of living in peace with ourselves are indistinguishable from those that enable us to live in peace with others. It is not only a training for a harmonious life in society, but is also a training that very often requires that we live with others. We shall deal with this later.

9.   A. Maslow, *Vers une Psychologie de l'Etre*, Paris, Fayard, 1972.

10.   M. Gorbachev, *Perestroika*, New York, Harper & Row, 1987; New York, Fontana, 1988.

Methods of education

We recall that the fundamental theory of the process of the destruction of peace and of the process of the creation of the vicious circle of compulsive repetition characteristic of the 'neurosis of paradise lost' provokes a sufficiently strong motivation to search for a means of escaping the vicious circle and to learn the techniques which foster the attainment of inner peace.

In fact the description in the previous section is full of suggested methods. We return to the subject only to mention which methods to develop in the short-, medium- and long-term programmes.

Short-term programme

In the 'Art of Living in Peace' workshop, the educational methods are divided up in the following manner, in line with the scheme mentioned previously:

- *Preliminary session:* initial motivation of participants and creating a warm and happy atmosphere (dancing and questions).
- *Past, present and future of humanity:* use of brainstorming to make an assessment of past, present and future, and also to create an awareness of the enormous gap that separates human ideals of peace from reality, now or in the past.
- *Obstacles to peace:* brief summary of the fundamental theory of the process of the destruction of peace.
- *Being at peace with oneself:* the origin of the neurosis of paradise lost (theory and dramatization); peace of the body (relaxation and nutritional advice); peace of the heart (becoming aware of destructive emotions; visualizing a new constructive project; psychotherapies; heart qualities and how to awaken them); peace of mind (how to move beyond fragmentation; dancing and life; meditation; peak experiences; towards a scale of 'constructive' values).

Medium- and long-term programme

The above programme can be undertaken in detail, with the help of good professionals or masters of the various disciplines mentioned in the text (relaxation, yoga, meditation, tai chi), health and nutrition counsellors, and therapists of various persuasions.

One could also add some of the new co-operative games[11] and peace games that have been created by the Findhorn Community.[12]

---

11.   P. Weil, op.cit., p. 107-12.
12.   D. N. Lefevre, *Jeux Nouveaux*, Barret-le-Bas, Le Souffle d'Or, 1988.

Table 5. Values and behaviour

CLASSIFICATION OF VALUES	VALUES	BEHAVIOUR	
		CONSTRUCTIVE	DESTRUCTIVE
TRANSPERSONAL	Union The sacred Wisdom Grace Bliss Fulfilment Wholeness	Harmony Non-duality	Division Judgement Wariness
KNOWLEDGE	Knowing Clarity Truth Justice	Meditation Reflection Self-discovery Equanimity	Ignorance Lying Hiding
INSPIRATION	Creativity Beauty	Imagination Intuition Trust Creativity Openness	Closedness
LOVE	Altruism Humanism Harmony Tenderness	Understanding Empathy Help	Rancour Selfishness Resentment
POWER	Equanimity Autonomy	Co-operation Freedom of speech	Domination Dependence
SENSUALITY	Pleasure	Sharing	Possessiveness Attachment
SECURITY	Freedom of body Health Existence Basic comfort	Respect Non-violence Courage Peace	Violence Aggression Allowing killing Infection Pollution

In addition to the psychotherapies, a long-term programme can be an excellent opportunity for initiation into the spiritual traditions to which the Declarations of Venice and Vancouver refer.

Chapter 2

The art of living in peace with others

Pathogenic consensus and social expression of energy

The contemporary 'normosis'

We have already seen how a lack of harmony causes us to create a society that is violent, pathological and in its turn pathogenic in its relation to the individual, to such an extent that we find we are prisoners in a closed system where nobody knows where things start: in the individual or in society.

One could even say that the majority of opinions, attitudes and behaviours about which there is a general consensus and which dictate what is 'normal', in reality lead us to a 'normosis', because in effect these agreements are social pressures which force the individual, in one way or another, to 'adapt' to abnormal rules.

Among these pathogenic and aberrant consensus we find the concept of 'fair war', which even has solid support in law. Once war has been legally declared, we acquire the right to kill all our enemies. In the name of this 'normal' principle, we train the young men throughout the world – this youth which basically desires only peace – to kill their fellow humans, during their 'normally' obligatory period of military service.

A similar consensus existed in the past concerning duelling to avenge one's damaged honour. This practice is today considered illegal, outmoded and even ridiculous. When will war be outlawed, as duelling was? Is it not in fact a collective duel? Will the world take this same evolutionary step with regard to violence and war?

It is this that we are working towards. To that end, we must help humanity escape from its 'normosis', to develop the full awareness that will prevent people from adapting to consensus and rules that are in fact pathological, even though they are statistically 'normal'.

In this respect it is just as important to work on the social level as on the individual level and, if possible, both simultaneously.

The three social manifestations of energy

In the area of society, characterized by the social sciences, we have quite a number of research projects and programmes of action concerned with war, violence and peace, although this is not the place to go into them in great detail. There are available in the educational field some excellent summaries of this work, especially relating to the social and international levels.[1]

We are going to classify them according to our non-fragmented model which energy manifests itself at the social level in three forms.

Culture

This corresponds at an energy level to human and universal intelligence, and is the domain of anthropology and legal studies.

It consists of the sum total of the consensus, opinions, attitudes, feelings, perspectives, concepts, stereotypes, prejudices and laws of any given society. It is culture that dictates the habits and behaviour of this society. It is expressed through art in its various forms, through philosophy, scientific knowledge and spiritual values, and is passed on through social institutions such as the family, schools and public and private organizations.

Society

This corresponds at the energy level to human and universal life and its principal science is sociology.

Society consists of the sum total of relationships, interactions and communications between individuals, groups and institutions. It is expressed by means of, or within social institutions such as the family, schools, universities, businesses and governmental and non-governmental organizations.

1. UNESCO, *Education for International Co-operation and Peace at the Primary School Level*, Paris, UNESCO, 1983; C. Wulf et al., *Handbook of Peace Education.* Frankfurt, IPRA, 1974; E. Boulding, *The Child and Non-Violent Social Change,* ibid., p. 101–35.

Economy

This corresponds at the energy level to the human body and universal matter. It is the domain of the economic sciences.

It refers to the production, distribution and consumption or use of habitat or territory, of food, clothing and wealth of any kind, including money and its circulation.

It functions through the individual worker or private and public organizations.

Education for peace

For each of these groups (which are closely linked) we shall now describe the various methods and educational techniques that have been recommended as solutions during the course of the past fifty years.

We can distinguish three types of education for social and international peace: cultural education for peace, social education for peace and economic education for peace.

Since there have been a considerable number of suggested solutions, we limit ourselves here to a simple listing of them accompanied by some essential comments.

At a cultural level

In the context of the year 2000, which the United Nations proclaimed 'International Year for the Culture of Peace', UNESCO launched the Manifesto 2000, accessible via the Internet, which so far has gathered over 74 million commitments to a personal contribution for peace.

We live in a culture of violence but there are more and more of us who want to bring about a culture of peace 'so that today's ideal may become tomorrow's reality'.[2]

The United Nations' decision to devote the next decade 'Decade for the Culture of Peace and Non-violence for the Benefit of the Children of the World' can only support and reinforce this deep aspiration in each human being's heart.

At the level on which we have defined it, it is possible to draw attention to numerous educational initiatives aimed at changing concepts, opinions, feelings and values. As Johan Galtung has shown,[3] the

2.   A. B. Jakumar, at the opening session of the 6th World Congress for Education for Peace at UNESCO, Paris, July 2000.
3.   J. Galtung, 'On Peace Education', *Handbook of Peace Education*, p.169, op. cit.

goal is to transform the values relating to the world we reject and that we no longer want, into those of a world we prefer.

The main educational techniques currently recommended or used are as follows.

The teaching and promulgation of the International Charter of Human Rights[4]

A look at the ratification of the principal international tools for promoting human rights[5] shows us to what extent the efforts of the United Nations have put values linked with human rights on to the agenda of almost every country in the world. To a large extent this is the result of a huge educational campaign.

UNESCO has published a guide for teaching human rights at all levels and in different kinds of education.[6] In the Preface, G. B. Kutukdjian gives a general idea of 'the great lessons to be drawn from the educational work of these past years' and states that 'perhaps the study of human rights is not a supplementary subject to add to the curriculum, because in essence it is reflection and research . . . on concrete and tangible social relationships. Henceforth the teaching of human rights – training for democracy (rights, duties and obligations) – will become education for freedom and solidarity.'[7]

This UNESCO publication contains some valuable pointers for programmes and educational principles which can be used as a basis for teaching human rights at university level, in primary or secondary education, and in community education. It also contains a bibliography on human rights education.

Cultural education for peace through the mass media

The press, newspapers, magazines, radio, television and advertising are, as we well know, vehicles of enormous power for the promulgation of values of peace. Numerous studies have been carried out into the role of the mass media in encouraging violence in the world.

---

4.   United Nations, *Human Rights – The International Charter of Human Rights*, New York, United Nations, 1988.
5.   'State of Ratification of the Main International Instruments Relating to Human Rights on 1 January 1990', *International Dimension of Human Rights*, Appendix 1, Greenwood Press/UNESCO, 1982.
6.   *Teaching Human Rights*, Paris, UNESCO, 1986, Vol. V.
7.   G. B. Kutukdjian, op. cit., p. 1-2.

In his introduction to the UNESCO publication *Violence and Terror in the Mass Media*[8] George Gerbner states that violence and terror in the mass media give social relationships a conflicting image; they show how force can be used to control, isolate, dominate, provoke or destroy. Some of the research cited shows that the percentage of violent content has increased considerably in television programmes and now affects more than half of all programmes.

The studies carried out on the educational role that the mass media should play are already numerous. There is a summary of them in a UNESCO publication entitled *Media Education*.[9] In fact the mass media constitute a fourth power in society, the scale of which we are only just beginning to become aware. To state that it should take on an educational role because of its power is not enough. If we are to believe Michel Souchon, in his conclusion to the above-mentioned publication, extremely strong trends mark the history of relationships between the educational world and that of the mass media. Among these trends he points out the use of the media for purposes of entertainment, the restriction and uneven distribution of financial resources, and out-moded techniques of education, which are not well-suited to the demands of the media. Reconciliation between education and the media is possible, however,[10] and there are indications that it is happening in several countries. That, at least, is desirable.

Other educational approaches relating to a culture of peace

The subject is so vast that here we can only touch lightly on the various perspectives, each one of which, nevertheless, merits a detailed presentation and which are in fact the objects of educational studies and practices. Among others, we mention:

*   Libraries dedicated to peace and the introduction of the subject into existing libraries.
*   The study and promulgation of a global history of peace which would be a means of balancing the tendency of school textbooks to provide only obvious facts relating to battles, victories and defeats.

8.   G. Gerbner, 'Introduction', *Violence and Terror in the Media*, Paris, UNESCO, 1989 (Studies and Information Documents, No. 102).
9.   A. Moles, *Media Education*, Paris, UNESCO, 1984.
10. M. Souchon, 'Education and the Mass Media: Contradictions and Convergences', *Media Education*, p. 374 ff,.Paris, UNESCO, 1984.

- The education of soldiers for peace, beginning with the introduction in military academies of courses on the role of the military in the preservation of peace and strategies for transforming military service into civil service in countries that constitute economic or political communities, such as the European Union, on condition that the same is done in every country in the world.[11]

- Education for disarmament is a related aspect. The World Congress on Education for Disarmament lists the essential points of this kind of education and recommends that students develop a critical judgement regarding steps taken to reduce armaments and to eliminate war as 'an internationally acceptable practice'.[12]

- Legal education for peace in law schools.

- The development of an organizational holistic cultural movement in business and in governmental and non-governmental organizations, starting with the various branches of the United Nations. This culture would take into consideration human beings, production and sufficiency – that is indispensable for peace.

- The development of the exchange and intercultural correspondence movement for young people all over the world.

'All human beings inseparably belong to the human family and depend on one another for their existence, well-being and development.'[13]

At a social level

The establishment of peace at the social level depends not only on individual education for peace, as we discussed earlier, but also on direct action on human interpersonal relationships, between different groups and nations.

To this end several methods have been developed, especially after the Second World War. We mention a few:

- Group dynamics in its various forms: training groups, encounter groups, intergroup workshops, directing meetings, management leadership training, psycho-sociological intervention. The main purpose of these techniques is to identify and work on, in a

11. Conclusions of the 'Soldiers for Peace' seminar held in April 1990 at the City of Peace Foundation, International Holistic University of Brasilia (not published).

12. UNESCO, *UNESCO Yearbook on Peace and Conflict Studies*, p. 118-21, Paris, UNESCO, 1987.

13. *Declaration of Human Responsibilities for Peace and Sustainable Development*, Article 4, Chapter II, Costa Rica, United Nations University of Peace, 1989.

real-life situation, obstacles to communication and causes of conflict. Set in motion by the studies of Kurt Lewin and the work of the National Training Laboratories of Bethel (NTL), there are now innumerable variations of this method.

- Having identical objectives are psychodrama, sociodrama, role-playing and sociometry created by J. L. Moreno. The applications of these to social education for peace are considerable.

- Non-competitive games and sports stimulate co-operation, as discussed earlier.

- Peace strategy games, simulations of international peace strategies, allow us to forecast to a certain extent the reactions of enemies; for example taking the initiative to make an important unilateral reduction in weapons can encourage the other side to do the same, as has already been the case.

- Martial arts such as aikido and Japanese judo foster a calm state of mind and respect for one's opponent as well as an awareness of what is happening at an energy level within oneself and with others.

At the political level an attempt to create peace could be developed through the organization of conferences and meetings where politicians could together make a study of what unites them beyond their ideological differences.

At the religious level these last thirty years have been a witness to ecumenical meetings, conferences and seminars of remarkable quality, contributing to and fostering reconciliation and understanding between the representatives of the various spiritual traditions.

What is important about all the above methods is that we re-learn respect for the essence of each of our fellow human beings.

At an economic level

As long as there is poverty, hunger, disease, infant mortality, overpopulation and the abandonment of millions of children in the streets, it will not be possible to attain peace either in our consciousness, or in our national or international relationships.

In fact, for reasons that we are unable to discuss here, but which originate in the fantasy of separation and possessiveness, existing economic systems have only partially solved this problem.

In order for there to be economic education for peace, we need an economic theory of peace that takes into consideration individual, social and ecological concomitance – in other words, a new holistic economy that integrates and goes beyond the positive contributions of current economic systems.

The globalization process reveals certain hugely destructive tendencies in today's economy. Growing social inequality and exclusion, the thoughtless exploitation of the resources and populations of the Third World and snowballing environmental disasters are all warnings of more or less imminent danger. They highlight the need to create new economic models.

The citizens and organizations which are becoming aware of the seriousness of the situation, and also of their creative potential to redirect positively socio-economic evolution, are growing in number. This has recently given rise to various initiatives such as the following:

- The reintroduction of bartering as a means of economic exchange within small communities that are developing in France and Belgium known as SEL (Système d'échange local: Local Exchange System) and LETS (Local Exchange Trading Systems) in Anglo-Saxon countries.

- The formation of various responsible consumer networks (RCR).

- The development of the socially responsible companies network (Social Venture Network).

- The creating of ethical labels to identify companies that practise fair trading, including the Ethibel label.

- The emergence of alternative banks that operate with an ethical use of money such as the Triodos Bank in Belgium and the Netherlands.

- A movement in favour of a universal benefit that aims to provide all the citizens of the planet with a guaranteed minimum income.

- The work of the Lisbon Group that draws attention to the risks of globalization.

It will take interdisciplinary teams working both theoretically and experimentally to create that theory and to formulate recommendations for the various countries of the world based on research into economic solutions and taking into account the five 'E's recommended by Pierre Danserau, namely: ecology, ethology, economy in its true sense, ethnology and ethics.[14]

In the meantime, while paying attention to the attempts at innovation in progress, we shall continue to publish critical analyses of the

14. P. Danserau, *La Terre des Hommes et le Paysage Interieur*, p. 143 ff, Ottawa, Lemeac, 1973, and following.

war-fostering aspects of current economic systems. There are studies which meet this need.[15] It goes without saying that all educational methods can be used to this end. Johan Galtung, for example, suggests the use of dramatization to play out the effects of the different socio-economic systems.

We shall also promulgate and encourage movements and attitudes likely to remedy the current situation, such as those founded on the notions of basic comfort, voluntary simplicity and sustainable development.

Basic well-being

Another problem facing the most underprivileged as well as developing countries is that of basic well-being.

To define basic well-being is not simple because it depends on the economic level of each population; it is not the same for a European as for an Indian. Nevertheless, we can agree on one thing. All human beings need wholesome and sufficient nourishment to maintain their health, and they need shelter against bad weather and clothes to protect them from extremes of temperature.

Will we get there one day? The answer belongs to the future though humanity seems to already possess the necessary means to achieve this.

Voluntary simplicity

This is a movement sparked by E. F. Schumacher in his book *Small is Beautiful*[16] and amplified under this title by Duane Elgin.[17] The originator of this expression, Richard Gregg, defined it in the following way:

'Voluntary simplicity applies to internal and external conditions alike. It involves purity of intention, sincerity and honesty towards oneself, as well as the avoidance of outer complications, of having lots of trivial possessions as our main purpose for living. It means organizing our energy and our desires, partly restricting ourselves in some aspects of life to ensure a greater abundance of life in other ways. This implies a conscious organization of our life towards a meaningful goal.'

15.   See, for example, the study by Jurgen Markstahler, Volker Wagner and Dieter Sanghaas, 'Structural Dependence and Underdevelopment', *Handbook of Peace Education*, op. cit., p. 185.

16.   E. F. Schumacher, *Small is Beautiful*, London, Vintage, 1993.

17   D. Elgin, *Voluntary Simplicity*, New Jersey, William Morrow, 1988.

Voluntary simplicity is a life style whose essence can be summed up in five points:

- Material simplicity through relinquishing unnecessary consumption and choosing to live with the bare essentials.
- The human scale by creating work premises and community centres that are small enough to promote a genuine closeness between people as well as more efficient control of possible economic, social and environmental imbalances.
- A spirit of independence which encourages people to depend as little as possible on the consumer society by developing one's own resources and abilities both manually and intellectually.
- Ecological awareness which encourages one to become an ally of nature rather than an exploiter.
- Self-development, based on seeking cultural and spiritual values rather than a thirst for power or the accumulation of material goods. This would lead to a redefinition of professional motivation in terms of service and the achievement of one's deep aspirations.

It seems that several million people in the developed countries are practising, more or less completely, this new way of living. But in the still-developing countries, the opposite problem presents itself, that of basic well-being.

Sustainable development

According to renowned research scientists, if the current rate of wastage, pollution or destruction of forests is maintained, the world's social and economic system will not survive.

Sustainable development stresses the need to envisage economic development with a long-term approach and respect for the individual and social ecology, and without destruction of the environment.

To this end, when we think about the costs of growth and progress it is vital that we bear in mind what the senseless pillaging of the world's natural resources, pollution and the destruction of the environment cost the community in terms of violence and conflict, non-respect of social justice or the fundamental rights of each human being as recognized by the Declaration of Human Rights.

We are beginning to realize to what extent the economy can at times trigger social and economic disasters when its agenda is solely profit, competitiveness, efficiency and short-term profitability.

The application of this sustainable development principle to economics could condition the future of the planet and future generations.

Methods of education

Short-term programme

We present here an outline of the techniques used in our 'Art of Living in Peace' workshop, as far as they concern living in peace with others.

We shall not go into them in great detail as we do not want to detract from the effects that people experience from encountering them for the first time and also because some of the techniques must be undertaken by educators themselves so that they can understand their importance and the way they work. Just reading about them is not recommended and would not have any effect.

The process of the destruction of social ecology

- Brief reminder of the process of destruction of inner harmony and its repercussions on social harmony. The destruction of peace on the cultural, social and economic level.
- Experience of group dynamics with regard to concepts and prejudices: what it is that divides the group and what unites it.

Rebuilding peace in society

At the cultural level, we shall look at:

- The Universal Declaration of Human Rights (reading and discussion).
- Universal values (review and comments).

At the social level, the subjects covered are:

- The causes of war and peace (discussion of texts).
- Education for peace (comments).
- Spiritual interaction (group experience).
- Humankind around the planet (visualization with sound-track).

At an economic level, through reading and discussing texts, we shall examine:

- Basic comfort.
- Voluntary simplicity.
- New professional motivation.
- Sustainable development.

Medium- and long-term programme

The basic text for this module makes numerous suggestions. Collaboration with psycho-sociologists, sociologists, anthropologists and economists will, without doubt, be of great assistance.

The same plan as indicated for a short-term programme can be followed.

Here are some suggested sources for research and additional consultation:

DIDIER, P.-F. *Guide Pratique de la Paix Mondiale.* Paris, Marval, 1985. This work contains a source of inspiration in the form of 38 'levers' for peace.

FERENCZ, B. B.; KEYES Jr, K. *Planethood, The Key to Your Future.* Preface by Robert Muller. Love Line Books, 1991.

M'BOW, M. A. et al. *Consensus and Peace.* Paris, UNESCO, 1980.

MARQUIER, A.; DUMONT, V. *Le Défi de l'Humanité.* Knowlton (Quebec), Les Editions Universelles de Verseau, 1987.

MULLER, R. *Nouvelle Genèse. Vers une Spiritualité Globale.* Knowlton (Quebec), Les Editions Universelles de Verseau, 1990.

UNESCO. *UNESCO Yearbook on Peace and Conflict Studies.* Paris, UNESCO, yearly.

Chapter 3

The art of living in peace with the environment

Human nature and the nature of the environment

The environment is an expression of universal energy. As human beings we are an integral part of it. Moreover, we are made of this energy and as a consequence we integrate it within ourselves.

As we saw previously, the loss of this notion of inseparability between humans and nature lies at the root of our destruction of the environment.

To train others in the art of living in peace with nature involves before all else re-establishing in human beings this holistic vision of their unseverable connection with nature.

Starting with the personal egocentric consciousness, broadening out into anthropocentric social consciousness and moving on to a geo-centric planetary consciousness, humankind will have to discover a transpersonal and universal cosmic consciousness.

As we suggested above, the non-fragmentary theory of energy allows us to provide models for understanding the nature of things and to clearly classify the great problems that afflict the human race, as well as to propose solutions for recovering our lost peace.

Towards a method of ecological education

This non-fragmentary theory of energy also offers the possibility, at the level of the relationship between humans and their environment, of establishing a method of education that helps humankind become aware that its own nature and the nature of the universe are in essence the same.

The immediate consequence of this is that we will come to the obvious conclusion that all thought followed by actions that harm the environment will, directly or indirectly, in the short or long term, affect ourselves or our descendants. It makes us co-responsible for the preservation of the environment.

This, then, is clearly the essential objective of a method of ecological education, which would be part of a curriculum that follows the three main manifestations of energy. Although we discussed these earlier, we shall summarize them here.

The three forms of manifestation of energy in the natural world are matter, life and information. As they are varying manifestations of one energy, they are obviously indivisible to the extent that they are represented within each other, as in a hologram.

Moreover, we can say that there is life in matter, composed of solid, liquid, fiery and gaseous elements, according to so-called physical laws, which are its informational aspect. In this sense matter is intelligent.

In the same way, we can state that life originates from matter and obeys what we call biological laws. Life implies the existence of information; everything takes place as if life itself were intelligent and wise. Information does not evade this three-in-one aspect since its transmission depends on physical systems in all the processes of communication, and communication itself is a vital process that finds its ultimate expression in love.

Information is the expression of laws of wisdom that are part of the implicate order of the universe as David Bohm describes.[1] In this sense the nature of the universe and the universe of nature would be a thought full of love. Here we reach the frontier where perhaps poetry and the real world merge and where the universe takes on a psychological aspect, although without implying an anthropomorphic projection. On the contrary, humankind would only be a reflection of this psychocosmological aspect of the universe; if there is any projection, it would be that of nature within humans.

So, let us again take the three-in-one concept of energy and examine its educational forms for giving humans the opportunity to become aware in themselves of their fundamental inseparability from the environment. This implies, on the epistemological level, the acceptance of the idea of the indivisibility of physics, biology and psychology.

In the same way, inner ecology, social ecology and planetary ecology all constitute only one ecology.

1.   D. Bohm, *The Undivided Universe,* London, Routledge.

'The recognition by a human being that he is part of the same process that defines the universe enhances his self-image and allows him to transcend egoism, which is the principal threat to his own long-term interests and to the environment and, in consequence, to his future.'[2]

The most direct way of achieving this purpose is to make each human being aware of the correspondence that exists between his/her own structure and vital or psychic systems, and the structure and vital or cybernetic systems of the universe. In other words, the correspondence between his/her inner world and his/her outer world, between himself/herself as subject, and the universe as object.

It is obvious that educators will themselves have to be deeply convinced of this correspondence and of the kind of illusion in which the majority of humankind is caught, before wanting to encourage such a vision in others.

The method of ecological education will also have to educate trainees or students in how to preserve the environment.

Now we shall look at these three aspects of ecological education, namely:

• Ecological education about matter.
• Ecological education about information.
• Ecological education about information.

About matter

As recommended by Pierre Dansereau, it is sensible to start with matter in relation to any analysis of ecosystems, in the sense of so-called in-organic matter.[3] In his ecosystem model, this renowned ecologist distinguishes the following six levels: mineral, vegetable, herbivorous animals, carnivorous animals, the level of investment and that of control.

In the energetic flow, minerals are absorbed by plants; plants are eaten by herbivores, who themselves provide food for carnivores; moreover, at every level we can notice investments by plants, animals and human beings aimed at accumulating reserves; on the latter level we find the will and planning that corresponds to Teilhard de Chardin's noosphere.[4]

2. *Vancouver Declaration on Survival into the 21st Century*, UNESCO, 15 September 1989.
3. P. Dansereau, *op. cit.*, p. 84–9.
4. P. Teilhard de Chardin, *Le Phénomène Humain*, Paris, Seuil, 1955.

So we start with a method of ecological education in relation to matter. Our experience tells us that the best way to awaken a consciousness of the non-separation between humans and inorganic matter is to use every possible form of demonstration of the correspondence between the body and matter. It is also possible to help people understand and become aware of the correspondence between the 'outer' and the 'inner', in relation to the earth, the soil, water, fire in the form of light and heat, the atmosphere and the air, and even the space-energy of which everything is ultimately made. This can be done by theoretical studies, research activities and visualization. The same methods are applied to plant and animal life.

'The concept of an organic macrocosm recaptures the rhythms of life. These rhythms can help human beings reintegrate with nature and restore their relationship with others in space and in time.'[5]

About life

Then we shall explore the same processes as far as they concern the plant and animal dimensions. It is relatively easy for students to understand that there is life in both themselves and the universe, and that it is all one life.

A comparative analysis of human, plant and animal evolution encourages and reinforces this work.

About information

Relating information and the intelligence directing the ecosystems by means of human intelligence and thought, and the demonstration of the existence of a wisdom immanent in human beings and nature can initially give rise to certain theoretical or even ideological objections. That is why the demonstration must be based on a rigorous observation of facts, leaving each student free to make his or her own analogies and conclusions in relation to this subject.

For example, deep reflection on a seed, on the blueprint for a tree that does not yet exist, and comparison with a mental project, that is, the idea of a hut that does not yet exist, constitutes among other methods quite a good means of creating awareness on the subject.[6]

---

5. *Vancouver Declaration on Survival into the 21st Century*, UNESCO, 15 September 1989.
6. Transpersonal psychology has been at the root of many encounters between physicists, on the one hand, and psychologists and representatives of the great spiritual traditions, on the other.

Creating awareness regarding the protection
of the environment

The fact that human beings are becoming aware of their nature and that they are one with nature is leading them inevitably to become concerned with the preservation of their environment.

Certain universities are taking a growing interest in this question and their programmes will serve as a source of inspiration. In addition, the report of the World Commission on Environment and Development, known as the Brundtland Report, is also a source of inspiration for curricula,[7] while UNESCO's 'Man and Biosphere' (MAB) programme provides information that can be used in formulating courses and educational and training methods.[8]

But as our study is centred on peace, the aim of ecological education for peace is obviously not to train specialists in the environment, but to make the majority of educators – and through them the population of the Earth – aware of their contribution and individual responsibility with regard to the environment. That is why our first section of suggestions relating to the diminution or even dissolution of the fantasy of separation is so important. They are effective in awakening an attitude of profound respect towards the planet. This we begin to perceive as an extension of ourselves, to which we are linked by an umbilical cord, as invisible as the air which links us to it.

What is needed, then, is to complete this process of creating awareness with recommendations on the effective contribution that each individual can bring to this field. Lists of specific actions exist in numerous publications.[9] The subject of nutrition can be a good starting-point for demonstrating the relationship between the environment and ourselves.[10]

The Declaration of Human Responsibilities for Peace and Sustainable Development, issued by the United Nations University of Peace, is a document which should be made an obligatory part of this type of curriculum, for it provides a theoretical and ethical support not

7.   *Our Common Future,* Oxford/NewYork, Oxford University Press, 1987.
8.   *Man Belongs to the Earth,* p. 115–26, Paris, UNESCO, 1988.
9.   *Guide d'Action Personnelle pour la Terre,* New York, 1989 (Projet de transmission du Programme de l'environnement des Nations Unies); P.-F. Didier, *Guide Pratique de la Paix Mondiale,* p. 70–7, Paris, Marval, 1985.
10.   J. Robbins, *Diet For a New America,* Stillpoint, 1990; P. Desbrosses, *Le Krach Alimentaire,* Editions du Rocher, 1988 (Préface de l'Abbé Pierre).

only within the scope of this current module, but also for the principal ideas which we have developed throughout this book.[11]

Methods of education

Short-term programme

The 'Art of Living in Peace' workshop, the seminar devised by the International Holistic University of Brasilia, part of the City of Peace Foundation, constitutes, on the level of ecological education for peace, a means of providing people with permanent motivation for taking personal and effective action with regard to the environment.

Following is the basic outline of this planetary ecology education method.

The process of the destruction of the environment

Presentation on the loss of the notion of interdependence and re-establishment of harmony with the environment (verbal presentation).

Peace with nature

- Presentation on establishing harmony with the environment.
- Matter: Journey into external and internal matter; visualization on the themes of earth, water, fire, air and space-energy.
- Life: outer and inner. Where do we come from? Where are we? Where are we going? A real-life experience of nature, done in pairs.
- Information: Intelligence seen from the outside and from the inside. Concentration and reflection on a seed and on the process of thought.

The dissolution of the fantasy of separation

Summary of the phases of dissolution in the form of a talk.

Project for contributing personally to peace with the environment

It is important that the training should end with a firm resolution to make a contribution to peace and to ecology, and that for each person

---

11. *Declaration of Human Responsibilities for Peace and Sustainable Development,* United Nations University of Peace, Costa Rica, 1989.

this resolution should be reinforced and accompanied by an individual plan of action, rooted in daily life.

- What I have done and what I am currently doing for peace and the environment. Each person makes a list of past and present actions.
- What I can and want to do in the immediate future and in the medium term for peace with the environment.
- Brainstorming in small groups, followed by mini-group exchanges and final decisions.
- Visualization of a specific situation in the near future.

Medium- and long-term programme

As well as everything that has been said so far about organizing a curriculum, the work undertaken may be continued according to the same model, including for example:

- More extensive documentation on the subject with the help of reading, films and video cassettes.
- Meetings with ecologists and environmental specialists.
- Exhibitions on the theme of the environment, organized by the students.
- Study and research groups in the field.
- Excursions and trips in groups.

As far as the individual practical action is concerned, 'Art of Living in Peace' circles, composed of about ten students at most, provide a framework for help and mutual support that helps to enhance each person's efforts.

Conclusion

I would like to finish this book by departing from what I see as a slightly over academic style to touch the heart of the reader directly.

This work is a synthesis of all that I have learned in my life in the West and in the East; yet I have gradually discovered that it also meets an urgent need among young people and the public at large, namely rediscovering the meaning of life.

The violence that threatens us wherever we are is one of the symptoms of the absence-of-meaning crisis that humanity is now faced with.

At the age of 33 I experienced the symptoms of this crisis physically. I had everything, more than I could have ever wished for and yet I felt deeply unhappy. Although I had studied psychology I could not grasp what was happening to me.

This crisis led me to a painful separation followed by cancer. A five-year period, during which I did not know whether I would survive, caused me to ask the essential questions, to reflect on the meaning of life: 'What am I doing on this planet?', 'What comes after death?', 'If there is nothing, this life is meaningless. And if there is something, what is it?'

That is when I learned how a crisis can be a major opportunity for transformation. To help myself I went into therapy, a very Western approach, and took up Yoga, which is typically Eastern. I then realized what the Venice Declaration was to recommend twenty years later in order to save the world from its fragmentation crisis: the meeting between East and West, which also corresponds to the reconciliation of the two hemispheres of our brain, the rational and the intuitive.

Today I am fully aware that the encounter is a far more significant one still: that of the male and female principle. I am convinced that the old paradigm that this book is about is, after all, an expression of an exclusively male vision that has dominated the world for over 4,000 years. The new paradigm stems from the awakening of the female principle. It integrates the two polarities in one vision and one common action.

We men have failed in our management of world affairs. It is now the couple's turn. If we want to save life on the planet we must unite the heart and the mind, feelings and thoughts, intuition and sensation in each of us.

I would like to say a few words more about the observations we have made as we have applied our 'Art of Living in Peace' pedagogical model.

Gradually, we have realized that the project far exceeded our expectations not only in terms of the enthusiasm it generated in those who have taken part in it, but also in terms of the various fields of application.

At the outset, the people taking part – sometimes specialists – cannot see the connection between violence and the possibility of transforming it into peace through education. For many people searching for peace has to do with the Middle East or Kosovo. It does not really concern them.

However, as violence in the world increases, the number of training institutes and educators who wish to follow an 'Art of Living in Peace' course is also growing and the same applies for teachers and in schools. We have also discovered a growing interest in this seminar on the part of companies and public bodies that offer it to their executives and staff in general as a result of the growing level of stress due to the rationalization of work and widespread down-sizing.

Another surprise was the request from the Brazilian police authorities to give all officers the 'Art of Living in Peace' seminar, which helped give them a better understanding of their work.

We have even tested this seminar in prisons, providing prisoners with an opportunity to discover that true peace lies within themselves through the realization that they could be prisoners of their emotions outside prison as well as free within themselves, albeit between four walls.

Finally, small conferences with a few practical demonstrations allow participants to get a better grasp of what we mean by the art of living in peace. These conferences often spark the desire to go on to follow the seminar.

By way of a conclusion, I would like to say that our emotion and satisfaction are great when we hear those taking part in our various seminars regularly saying the same thing: 'Thank you, it's really what I needed!' or 'This seminar has changed my way of being and the way I live!'

Appendices

Venice Declaration

Final Communiqué of the symposium 'Science and the Boundaries of Knowledge' Venice, 7 March 1986

The participants in the symposium 'Science and the Boundaries of Knowledge: the Prologue of our Cultural Past', organized by UNESCO in collaboration with the Giorgio Cini Foundation (Venice, 3-7 March 1986), in a spirit of open-mindedness and inquiry concerning today's values, have agreed on the following points:

1. We are witnessing a very important revolution in the field of science brought about by basic science (in particular by developments in physics and biology), by the upheavals it has wrought in logic, in epistemology and in everyday life through its technological applications. We note at the same time, however, a significant gap between a new world view emerging from the study of natural systems and the values that continue to prevail in philosophy, in the human and social sciences and in the life of modern society, values largely based on mechanistic determinism, positivism or nihilism. We believe that this discrepancy is harmful and indeed dangerous for the very survival of our species.

2. Scientific knowledge, on its own impetus, has reached the point where it can begin a dialogue with other forms of knowledge. In this sense, and while recognizing the fundamental differences between science and tradition, we see them as complementary rather than in contradiction. This new and mutually enriching exchange between science and the

different traditions of the world opens the door to a new vision of humanity, and even to a new rationalism, which could lead to a new metaphysical perspective.

3. While not wishing to attempt a global approach, nor to establish a closed system of thought, nor to invent a new utopia, we recognize the pressing need for truly transdisciplinary research through a dynamic exchange between the natural sciences, the social sciences, art and tradition. It could be said that this transdisciplinary mode is inherent in our brain through the dynamic interaction of its two hemispheres. Joint investigation of nature and of the imagination, of the universe and of man, might thus bring us closer to reality and enable us better to meet the various challenges of our time.

4. The conventional way of teaching science by a linear presentation of knowledge masks the divorce between today's science and world views which are outdated. We stress the need for new educational methods to take into account current scientific progress now coming into harmony with the great cultural traditions, the preservation and in-depth study of which appear essential. UNESCO would be the appropriate organization to promote such ideas.

5. The challenges of our time – the risk of destruction of our species, the impact of data processing, the implications of genetics, etc. – throw a new light on the social responsibilities of the scientific community, both in the initiation and application of research. Although scientists may have no control over the applications of their discoveries, they must not remain passive when confronted with the haphazard use of what they have discovered. It is our view that the magnitude of today's challenges requires, on the one hand, a reliable and steady flow of information to the public and, on the other hand, the establishment of multi- and transdisciplinary mechanisms for the guidance and even the carrying out of decision-making.

6. We hope that UNESCO will consider this encounter as a starting point and will encourage further reflection in a spirit of transdisciplinarity and universality.

We thank UNESCO for its initiative in organizing such a meeting according to its vocation for universality. We also thank the Giorgio Cini Foundation for allowing it to take place in an ideal location for this forum.

Signatories

D. A Akyeampong (Ghana), physicist-mathematician, University of Ghana.

Ubiratan D'Ambrosio (Brazil), mathematician, general faculty co-ordinator, Universadade Estadual de Campinas.

René Berger (Switzerland), honorary professor, University of Lausanne.

André Chouraqui (Israel).

Nicolo Dallaporta (Italy), honorary professor at the Ecole Internationale des Hautes Etudes in Trieste.

Pierre Dansereau (Canada).

Jean Dausset (France), Nobel Prize for Physiology and Medicine (1980), president of the Mouvement Universel de la Responsabilité Scientifique (MURS), France.

Maîtraye Devi (India), poet/writer.

Gilbert Durand (France), philosopher, founder of the Centre de Recherche sur l'Imaginaire.

Mahdi Elmandjra (Morocco).

Santaigo Genoves (Mexico), research scientist at the Anthropological Research Institute, resident academic at the National Medical Academy.

Susantha Goonatilake (Sri Lanka), research scientist, cultural anthropology.

Alexander King (United Kingdom).

Avishai Margalit (Israel), philosopher, Hebraic University of Jerusalem.

Eleonora Barbieri Masini (Italy).

Digby McLaren (Canada).

Yûjiro Nakamura (Japan), philosopher/writer, professor at the University of Meiji.

Basarab Nicolescu (France), physicist, CNRS.

Lisandro Otero (Cuba).

David Ottoson (Sweden), chairman of the Nobel Committee for physiology and medicine, professor and director, Karolinska Institute.

Michel Random (France), philosopher/writer.

Jacques G. Richardson (France/United States), writer, scientist.

Josef Riman (Czechoslovakia).

Abdus Salam (Pakistan), Nobel Prize for Physics (1979), director of the International Centre for Theoretical Physics, Trieste Italy – represented by Dr L. K. Shayo (Nigeria), mathematics professor.

Rupert Sheldrake (United Kingdom), Ph.D. in biochemistry, university of Cambridge.

Soedjatmoko (Indonesia).

Henry Stapp (United States), physicist, Lawrence Berkeley Laboratory, University of California, Berkeley.

David Suzuki (Canada), geneticist, University of British Columbia.

Charter of Transdisciplinarity

Adopted at the First World Congress of Transdisciplinarity, Convento da Arrábida, Portugal, 2–6 November 1994

Preamble

Whereas, the present proliferation of academic and non-academic disciplines is leading to an exponential increase of knowledge which makes a global view of the human being impossible;

Whereas, only a form of intelligence capable of grasping the cosmic dimension of the present conflicts is able to confront the complexity of our world and the present challenge of the spiritual and material self-destruction of the human species;

Whereas, life on earth is seriously threatened by the triumph of a techno-science that obeys only the terrible logic of productivity for productivity's sake;

Whereas, the present rupture between increasingly quantitative knowledge and increasingly impoverished inner identity is leading to the rise of a new brand of obscurantism with incalculable social and personal consequences;

Whereas, an historically unprecedented growth of knowledge is increasing the inequality between those who have and those who do not thus engendering increasing inequality within and between the different nations of our planet;

Whereas, at the same time, hope is the counterpart of all the afore-mentioned challenges, a hope that this extraordinary development of knowledge could eventually lead to an evolution not unlike the development of primates into human beings;

Therefore, in consideration of all the above, the participants of the First World Congress of Transdisciplinarity (Convento da Arrábida, Portugal, 2–6 November, 1994) have adopted the present Charter, which comprises the fundamental principles of the community of transdisciplinary researchers, and constitutes a personal moral commitment, without any legal or institutional constraint, on the part of everyone who signs this Charter.

Article 1

Any attempt to reduce the human being by formally defining what a human being is and subjecting the human being to reductive analyses within a framework of formal structures, no matter what they are, is incompatible with the transdisciplinary vision.

Article 2

The recognition of the existence of different levels of reality governed by different types of logic is inherent in the transdisciplinary attitude. Any attempt to reduce reality to a single level governed by a single form of logic does not lie within the scope of transdisciplinarity.

Article 3

Transdisciplinarity complements disciplinary approaches. It occasions the emergence of new data and new interactions from out of the encounter between disciplines. It offers us a new vision of nature and reality. Transdisciplinarity does not strive for mastery of several disciplines but aims to open all disciplines to that which they share and to that which lies beyond them.

Article 4

The keystone of transdisciplinarity is the semantic and practical unification of the meanings that traverse and lay beyond different disciplines. It presupposes an open-minded rationality by re-examining the concepts of 'definition' and 'objectivity'. An excess of formalism, rigidity of definitions and a claim to total objectivity, entailing the exclusion of the subject, can only have a life-negating effect.

Article 5

The transdisciplinary vision is resolutely open insofar as it goes beyond the field of the exact sciences and demands their dialogue and their re-conciliation with the humanities and the social sciences, as well as with art, literature, poetry and spiritual experience.

Article 6

In comparison with interdisciplinarity and multidisciplinarity, trans-disciplinarity is multireferential and multidimensional. While taking account of the various approaches to time and history, transdisciplinarity does not exclude a transhistorical horizon.

Article 7

Transdisciplinarity constitutes neither a new religion, nor a new philosophy, nor a new metaphysics nor a science of sciences.

Article 8

The dignity of the human being is of both planetary and cosmic dimensions. The appearance of human beings on Earth is one of the stages in the history of the universe. The recognition of the Earth as our home is one of the imperatives of transdisciplinarity. Every human being is entitled to a nationality, but as an inhabitant of the Earth is also a transnational being. The acknowledgement by international law of this twofold belonging, to a nation and to the Earth, is one of the goals of transdisciplinary research.

Article 9

Transdisciplinarity leads to an open attitude towards myths and religions and also towards those who respect them in a transdisciplinary spirit.

Article 10

No single culture is privileged over any other culture. The transdisciplinary approach is inherently transcultural.

Article 11

Authentic education cannot value abstraction over other forms of knowledge. It must teach contextual, concrete and global approaches. Transdisciplinary education revalues the role of intuition, imagination, sensibility and the body in the transmission of knowledge.

Article 12

The development of a transdisciplinary economy is based on the postulate that the economy must serve the human being and not the reverse.

Article 13

The transdisciplinary ethic rejects any attitude that refuses dialogue and discussion, regardless of whether the origin of this attitude is ideological, scientific, religious, economic, political or philosophical. Shared knowledge should lead to a shared understanding based on an absolute respect for the collective and individual otherness united by our common life in one and the same Earth.

Article 14

Rigour, openness, and tolerance are the fundamental characteristics of the transdisciplinary attitude and vision. Rigour in argument, taking into account all existing data, is the best defence against possible distortions. Openness involves an acceptance of the unknown, the unexpected and the unforeseeable. Tolerance implies acknowledging the right to ideas and truths opposed to our own.

Article final

The present Charter of Transdisciplinarity was adopted by the participants of the first World Congress of Transdisciplinarity, with no claim to any authority other than that of their own work and activity.

In accordance with procedures to be agreed upon by transdisciplinary minded persons of all countries, this Charter is open to the signature of anyone who is interested in promoting progressive national, international and transnational measures to ensure the application of these Articles in everyday life.

Convento da Arrábida, 6 November 1994
Editorial Committee
Lima de Freitas, Edgar Morin and Basarab Nicolescu

Declaration of Human Responsibilities for Peace and Sustainable Development

United Nations University of Peace, Costa Rica, 1989

Chapter I: Unity of the world

Article 1

Everything which exists is part of an interdependent universe. All living beings depend on one another for their existence, well-being and development.

Article 2

All human beings are an inseparable part of nature, upon which culture and human civilization have been built.

Article 3

Life on Earth is abundant and diverse. It is sustained by the unhindered functioning of natural systems which ensure the provision of energy, air, water and nutrients for all living creatures. Every manifestation of life on Earth is unique and essential and must therefore be respected and protected without regard to its apparent value to human beings.

Chapter II: Unity of the human family

Article 4

All human beings inseparably belong to the human family and depend on one another for their existence, well-being and development. Every human being is a unique expression and manifestation of life and has a personal contribution to make to life on Earth. Each human being has fundamental and inalienable rights and freedoms, without distinction of race, colour, sex, language, religion, political or other opinion, national or social origin, economic status or any other social situation.

Article 5

All human beings have the same basic needs and the same fundamental aspirations for their fulfilment. All individuals are the beneficiaries of the right to development, the purpose of which is to promote attainment of the full potential of each person.

Chapter III: The alternatives facing humanity, and universal responsibility

Article 6

Responsibility is an inherent aspect of any relation in which human beings are involved. This capacity to act responsibly in a conscious, independent, unique and personal manner is an inalienable creative quality of every human being. There is no limit to its scope or depth other than that established by each person for himself. The more it is acted upon and put into practice, the more it will grow and become strengthened.

Article 7

Of all living beings, human beings have the unique capacity to decide consciously whether to protect or harm the quality and conditions of life on Earth. In reflecting on the fact that they belong to the natural world and occupy a special position as participants in the evolution of natural processes, individuals can develop, on the basis of altruism, compassion and love, a sense of universal responsibility towards the world as an integral whole, towards the protection of nature, and towards the promotion of the highest evolutionary potential, with a view to creating these conditions which will enable them to achieve the highest level of spiritual and material well-being.

Article 8

At this critical time in history, human chances are crucial. In directing their actions toward the attainment of progress in society, human beings have frequently forgotten that they belong to the natural world, to an indivisible human family, and have overlooked their basic needs for a healthy life. Excessive consumption, abuse of the environment, and aggression between peoples have brought the natural processes of the Earth to a critical stage which threatens their survival. By reflecting on these issues, individuals will be able to discern their responsibility and, upon this basis, reorient their conduct towards peace and sustainable development.

Chapter IV: Reorientation towards peace and sustainable development

Article 9

When individuals recognize that all forms of life are unique and essential, that all human beings are the beneficiaries of the right to development, and that both peace and violence have their origins in the consciousness of persons, a sense of responsibility to act and think in a peaceful manner will develop. Through this peaceful consciousness, individuals will understand the nature of these conditions which are necessary for their well-being and development.

Article 10

Human beings who become conscious of their sense of responsibility towards the human family, the environment they inhabit, and of the need to think and act in a peaceful manner will realize their obligation to act in a way that is consistent with the observance of and respect for inherent human rights and will ensure that their consumption of resources is in keeping with the satisfaction of the basic needs of all.

Article 11

When members of the human family recognize that they are responsible to themselves and to present and future generations for the conservation of the planet, as protectors of the natural world and promoters of its continued development, they will realize their obligation to act in a rational manner in order to ensure the sustainability of life.

Article 12

Human beings have a continuing responsibility when setting up, taking part in or representing social units, corporations, and institutions, whether private or public. In addition, all such entities have a responsibility to promote peace and sustainability, and to put into practice the educational goals which are conducive to that end. These goals include fostering the consciousness of the interdependence of human beings among themselves and with nature, and awareness of the universal responsibility of individuals to solve the problems that they have engendered through their attitudes and actions, in a manner that is consistent with the protection of human rights and fundamental freedoms.

Let us be faithful to the privilege of our responsibility.

The four pillars
of education[1]

Pointers and recommendations

Education throughout life is based on four pillars: learning to know, learning to do, learning to live together and learning to be.

Learning to know, by combining a sufficiently broad general knowledge with the opportunity to work in depth on a small number of subjects. This also means learning to learn, so as to benefit from the opportunities education provides throughout life.

Learning to do, in order to acquire not only an occupational skill but also, more broadly, the competence to deal with many situations and work in teams. It also means learning to do in the context of young peoples' various social and work experiences which may be informal, as a result of the local or national context, or formal, involving courses, alternating study and work.

Learning to live together, by developing an understanding of other people and an appreciation of interdependence – carrying out joint projects and learning to manage conflicts – in a spirit of respect for the values of pluralism, mutual understanding and peace.

Learning to be, so as better to develop one's personality and be able to act with ever greater autonomy, judgement and personal responsibility. In that connection, education must not disregard any respect of

---

1.   Jacques Delors et al., *Learning: the Treasure Within,* Report to UNESCO of the International Commission on Education for the Twenty-first Century, 'Learning: the Treasure Within', UNESCO Publishing, 1996, 1998, p. 85.

a person's potential: memory, reasoning, aesthetic sense, physical capacities and communication skills.

Formal education systems tend to emphasize the acquisition of knowledge to the detriment of other types of learning; but it is vital now to conceive education in a more encompassing fashion. Such a vision should inform and guide future educational reforms and policy, in relation both to content and to methods.

United Nations General Assembly
Fifty third Session
Agenda Item 31
Adopted 13 September 1999

Declaration and Programme of Action on a Culture of Peace

Declaration on a Culture of Peace

The General Assembly,

Recalling the Charter of the United Nations, including the purposes and principles embodied therein,

Recalling also the Constitution of the United Nations Educational, Scientific and Cultural Organization, which states that 'since wars begin in the minds of men, it is in the minds of men that the defences of peace must be constructed',

Recalling further the Universal Declaration of Human Rights and other relevant international instruments of the United Nations system,

Recognizing that peace not only is the absence of conflict, but also requires a positive, dynamic participatory process where dialogue is encouraged and conflicts are solved in a spirit of mutual understanding and co-operation,

Recognizing also that the end of the Cold War has widened possibilities for strengthening a culture of peace,

Expressing deep concern about the persistence and proliferation of violence and conflict in various parts of the world,

Recognizing the need to eliminate all forms of discrimination and intolerance, including those based on race, colour, sex, language, religion, political or other opinion, national, ethnic or social origin, property, disability, birth or other status,

Recalling its resolution 52/15 of 20 November 1997, by which it proclaimed the year 2000 as the 'International Year for the Culture of Peace', and its resolution 53/25 of 10 November 1998, by which it proclaimed the period 2001–2010 as the 'International Decade for a Culture of Peace and Non-Violence for the Children of the World',

Recognizing the important role that the United Nations Educational, Scientific and Cultural Organization continues to play in the promotion of a culture of peace,

Solemnly proclaims the present Declaration on a Culture of Peace to the end that governments, international organizations and civil society may be guided in their activity by its provisions to promote and strengthen a culture of peace in the new millennium:

Article 1

A culture of peace is a set of values, attitudes, traditions and modes of behaviour and ways of life based on:

(a) Respect for life, ending of violence and promotion and practice of non-violence through education, dialogue and co-operation;

(b) Full respect for the principles of sovereignty, territorial integrity and political independence of states and non-intervention in matters which are essentially within the domestic jurisdiction of any state, in accordance with the Charter of the United Nations and international law;

(c) Full respect for and promotion of all human rights and fundamental freedoms;

(d) Commitment to peaceful settlement of conflicts;

(e) Efforts to meet the developmental and environmental needs of present and future generations;

(f) Respect for and promotion of the right to development;

(g) Respect for and promotion of equal rights and opportunities for women and men;

(h) Respect for and promotion of the right of everyone to freedom of expression, opinion and information;

(i) Adherence to the principles of freedom, justice, democracy, tolerance, solidarity, co-operation, pluralism, cultural diversity, dialogue and understanding at all levels of society and among nations; and fostered by an enabling national and international environment conducive to peace.

Article 2

Progress in the fuller development of a culture of peace comes about through values, attitudes, modes of behaviour and ways of life conducive to the promotion of peace among individuals, groups and nations.

Article 3

The fuller development of a culture of peace is integrally linked to:

(a) Promoting peaceful settlement of conflicts, mutual respect and understanding and international co-operation;

(b) Complying with international obligations under the Charter of the United Nations and international law;

(c) Promoting democracy, development and universal respect for and observance of all human rights and fundamental freedoms;

(d) Enabling people at all levels to develop skills of dialogue, negotiation, consensus-building and peaceful resolution of differences;

(e) Strengthening democratic institutions and ensuring full participation in the development process;

(f) Eradicating poverty and illiteracy and reducing inequalities within and among nations;

(g) Promoting sustainable economic and social development;

(h) Eliminating all forms of discrimination against women through their empowerment and equal representation at all levels of decision-making;

(i) Ensuring respect for and promotion and protection of the rights of children;

(j) Ensuring free flow of information at all levels and enhancing access thereto;

(k) Increasing transparency and accountability in governance;

(l) Eliminating all forms of racism, racial discrimination, xenophobia and related intolerance;

(m) Advancing understanding, tolerance and solidarity among all civilizations, peoples and cultures, including towards ethnic, religious and linguistic minorities;

(n) Realizing fully the right of all peoples, including those living under colonial or other forms of alien domination or foreign occupation, to self-determination enshrined in the Charter of the United Nations and embodied in the International Covenants on Human Rights, as well as in the Declaration on the Granting of Independence to Colonial Countries and Peoples contained in General Assembly resolution 1514 (XV) of 14 December 1960.

Article 4

Education at all levels is one of the principal means to build a culture of peace. In this context, human rights education is of particular importance.

Article 5

Governments have an essential role in promoting and strengthening a culture of peace.

Article 6

Civil society needs to be fully engaged in fuller development of a culture of peace.

Article 7

The educative and informative role of the media contributes to the promotion of a culture of peace.

Article 8

A key role in the promotion of a culture of peace belongs to parents, teachers, politicians, journalists, religious bodies and groups, intellectuals, those engaged in scientific, philosophical and creative and artistic activities, health and humanitarian workers, social workers, managers at various levels as well as to non-governmental organizations.

Article 9

The United Nations should continue to play a critical role in the promotion and strengthening of a culture of peace worldwide.

107th Plenary Meeting
13 September 1999

Programme of action on a culture of peace

The General Assembly,

Bearing in mind the Declaration on a Culture of Peace adopted on 13 September 1999,

    Recalling its resolution 52/15 of 20 November 1997, by which it proclaimed the year 2000 as the 'International Year for the Culture of Peace', and its resolution 53/25 of 10 November 1998, by which it proclaimed the period 2001–2010 as the 'International Decade for a Culture of Peace and Non-violence for the Children of the World';

    Adopts the following Programme of Action on a Culture of Peace.

Aims, strategies and main actors

1. The Programme of Action should serve as the basis for the International Year for the Culture of Peace and the International Decade for a Culture of Peace and Non-violence for the Children of the World.

2. Member States are encouraged to take actions for promoting a culture of peace at the national level as well as at the regional and international levels.

3. Civil society should be involved at the local, regional and national levels to widen the scope of activities on a culture of peace.

4. The United Nations system should strengthen its ongoing efforts to promote a culture of peace.

5. The United Nations Educational, Scientific and Cultural Organization should continue to play its important role in and make major contributions to the promotion of a culture of peace.

6. Partnerships between and among the various actors as set out in the Declaration should be encouraged and strengthened for a global movement for a culture of peace.

7. A culture of peace could be promoted through sharing of information among actors on their initiatives in this regard.

8. Effective implementation of the Programme of Action requires mobilization of resources, including financial resources, by interested governments, organizations and individuals.

Appendix 5

Strengthening actions at the national, regional and international levels by all relevant actors

9. Actions to foster a culture of peace through education:

(a) Reinvigorate national efforts and international co-operation to promote the goals of education for all with a view to achieving human, social and economic development and for promoting a culture of peace;

(b) Ensure that children, from an early age, benefit from education on the values, attitudes, modes of behaviour and ways of life to enable them to resolve any dispute peacefully and in a spirit of respect for human dignity and of tolerance and non-discrimination;

(c) Involve children in activities designed to instil in them the values and goals of a culture of peace;

(d) Ensure equality of access to education for women, especially girls;

(e) Encourage revision of educational curricula, including textbooks, bearing in mind the 1995 Declaration and Integrated Framework of Action on Education for Peace, Human Rights and Democracy for which technical co-operation should be provided by the United Nations Educational, Scientific and Cultural Organization upon request;

(f) Encourage and strengthen efforts by actors as identified in the Declaration, in particular the United Nations Educational, Scientific and Cultural Organization, aimed at developing values and skills conducive to a culture of peace, including education and training in promoting dialogue and consensus-building;

(g) Strengthen the ongoing efforts of the relevant entities of the United Nations system aimed at training and education, where appropriate, in the areas of conflict prevention and crisis management, peaceful settlement of disputes, as well as in post-conflict peace-building;

(h) Expand initiatives to promote a culture of peace undertaken by institutions of higher education in various parts of the world, including the United Nations University, the University for Peace and the project for twinning universities and the United Nations Educational, Scientific and Cultural Organization Chairs Programme.

10. Actions to promote sustainable economic and social development:

(a) Undertake comprehensive actions on the basis of appropriate strategies and agreed targets to eradicate poverty through national and international efforts, including through international co-operation;

(b) Strengthen the national capacity for implementation of policies and programmes designed to reduce economic and social inequalities within nations through, inter alia, international co-operation;

(c) Promote effective and equitable development-oriented and durable solutions to the external debt and debt-servicing problems of developing countries through, inter alia, debt relief;

(d) Reinforce actions at all levels to implement national strategies for sustainable food security, including the development of actions to mobilize and optimize the allocation and utilization of resources from all sources, including through international co-operation, such as resources coming from debt relief;

(e) Undertake further efforts to ensure that the development process is participatory and that development projects involve the full participation of all;

(f) Include a gender perspective and empowerment of women and girls as an integral part of the development process;

(g) Include in development strategies special measures focusing on needs of women and children as well as groups with special needs;

(h) Strengthen, through development assistance in post-conflict situations, rehabilitation, reintegration and reconciliation processes involving all engaged in conflicts;

(i) Incorporate capacity-building in development strategies and projects to ensure environmental sustainability, including preservation and regeneration of the natural resource base;

(j) Remove obstacles to the realization of the right of peoples to self-determination, in particular of peoples living under colonial or other forms of alien domination or foreign occupation, which adversely affect their social and economic development.

11. Actions to promote respect for all human rights:

(a) Full implementation of the Vienna Declaration and Programme of Action;

(b) Encouragement of development of national plans of action for the promotion and protection of all human rights;

(c) Strengthening of national institutions and capacities in the field of human rights, including through national human rights institutions;

(d) Realization and implementation of the right to development, as established in the Declaration on the Right to Development and the Vienna Declaration and Programme of Action;

(e) Achievement of the goals of the United Nations Decade for Human Rights Education (1995–2004);

(f) Dissemination and promotion of the Universal Declaration of Human Rights at all levels;

(g) Further support to the activities of the United Nations High Commissioner for Human Rights in the fulfilment of her or his mandate as established in General Assembly resolution 48/141 of 20 December 1993, as well as the responsibilities set by subsequent resolutions and decisions.

12. Actions to ensure equality between women and men:

(a) Integration of a gender perspective into the implementation of all relevant international instruments;

(b) Further implementation of international instruments that promote equality between women and men;

(c) Implementation of the Beijing Platform for Action adopted at the Fourth World Conference on Women, with adequate resources and political will, and through, inter alia, the elaboration, implementation and follow-up of the national plans of action;

(d) Promotion of equality between women and men in economic, social and political decision making;

(e) Further strengthening of efforts by the relevant entities of the United Nations system for the elimination of all forms of discrimination and violence against women;

(f) Provision of support and assistance to women who have become victims of any forms of violence, including in the home, workplace and during armed conflicts.

13. Actions to foster democratic participation:

(a) Reinforcement of the full range of actions to promote democratic principles and practices;

(b) Special emphasis on democratic principles and practices at all levels of formal, informal and nonformal education;

(c) Establishment and strengthening of national institutions and processes that promote and sustain democracy through, inter alia, training and capacity-building of public officials;

(d) Strengthening of democratic participation through, inter alia, the provision of electoral assistance upon the request of states concerned and based on relevant United Nations guidelines;

(e) Combating of terrorism, organized crime, corruption as well as production, trafficking and consumption of illicit drugs and money laundering, as they undermine democracies and impede the fuller development of a culture of peace.

14. Actions to advance understanding, tolerance and solidarity:

(a) Implement the Declaration of Principles on Tolerance and the Follow-up Plan of Action for the United Nations Year for Tolerance (1995);

(b) Support activities in the context of the United Nations Year of Dialogue among Civilizations in the year 2001;

(c) Study further the local or indigenous practices and traditions of dispute settlement and promotion of tolerance with the objective of learning from them;

(d) Support actions that foster understanding, tolerance and solidarity throughout society, in particular with vulnerable groups;

(e) Further support the attainment of the goals of the International Decade of the World's Indigenous People;

(f) Support actions that foster tolerance and solidarity with refugees and displaced persons, bearing in mind the objective of facilitating their voluntary return and social integration;

(g) Support actions that foster tolerance and solidarity with migrants;

(h) Promote increased understanding, tolerance and co-operation among all peoples through, inter alia, appropriate use of new technologies and dissemination of information;

(i) Support actions that foster understanding, tolerance, solidarity and co-operation among peoples and within and among nations.

15. Actions to support participatory communication and the free flow of information and knowledge:

(a) Support the important role of the media in the promotion of a culture of peace;

(b) Ensure freedom of the press and freedom of information and communication;

(c) Make effective use of the media for advocacy and dissemination of information on a culture of peace involving, as appropriate, the United Nations and relevant regional, national and local mechanisms;

(d) Promote mass communication that enables communities to express their needs and participate in decision-making;

(e) Take measures to address the issue of violence in the media, including new communication technologies, inter alia, the Internet;

(f) Increase efforts to promote the sharing of information on new information technologies, including the Internet.

16. Actions to promote international peace and security:

(a) Promote general and complete disarmament under strict and effective international control, taking into account the priorities established by the United Nations in the field of disarmament;

(b) Draw, where appropriate, on lessons conducive to a culture of peace learned from 'military conversion' efforts as evidenced in some countries of the world;

(c) Emphasize the inadmissibility of acquisition of territory by war and the need to work for a just and lasting peace in all parts of the world;

(d) Encourage confidence-building measures and efforts for negotiating peaceful settlements;

(e) Take measures to eliminate illicit production and traffic of small arms and light weapons;

(f) Support initiatives, at the national, regional and international levels, to address concrete problems arising from post-conflict situations, such as demobilization, reintegration of former combatants into society, as well as refugees and displaced persons, weapon collection programmes, exchange of information and confidence-building;

(g) Discourage the adoption of and refrain from any unilateral measure, not in accordance with international law and the Charter of the United Nations, that impedes the full achievement of economic and social development by the population of the affected countries, in particular women and children, that hinders their well-being, that creates obstacles to the full enjoyment of their human rights, including the right of everyone to a standard of living adequate for their health and well-being and their right to food, medical care and the necessary social services, while reaffirming that food and medicine must not be used as a tool for political pressure;

(h) Refrain from military, political, economic or any other form of coercion, not in accordance with international law and the Charter, aimed against the political independence or territorial integrity of any state;

(i) Recommend proper consideration for the issue of the humanitarian impact of sanctions, in particular on women and children, with a view to minimizing the humanitarian effects of sanctions;

(j) Promote greater involvement of women in prevention and resolution of conflicts and, in particular, in activities promoting a culture of peace in post-conflict situations;

(k) Promote initiatives in conflict situations such as days of tranquillity to carry out immunization and medicine distribution campaigns, corridors of peace to ensure delivery of humanitarian supplies and sanctuaries of peace to respect the central role of health and medical institutions such as hospitals and clinics;

(l) Encourage training in techniques for the understanding, prevention and resolution of conflict for the concerned staff of the United Nations, relevant regional organizations and Member States, upon request, where appropriate.

107th plenary meeting
13 September 1999

Manifesto 2000
for a culture of peace
and non-violence

Because the year 2000 must be a new beginning, an opportunity to transform – all together – the culture of war and violence into a culture of peace and non-violence.

Because this transformation demands the participation of each and every one of us, and must offer young people and future generations the values that can inspire them to shape a world based on justice, solidarity, liberty, dignity, harmony and prosperity for all.

Because the culture of peace can underpin sustainable development, environmental protection and the well-being of each person.

Because I am aware of my share of responsibility for the future of humanity, in particular to the children of today and tomorrow.

I pledge in my daily life, in my family, my work, my community, my country and my region, to:

• Respect the life and dignity of each human being without discrimination or prejudice;

• Practice active non-violence, rejecting violence in all its forms: physical, sexual, psychological, economical and social, in particular towards the most deprived and vulnerable such as children and adolescents;

• Share my time and material resources in a spirit of generosity to put an end to exclusion, injustice and political and economic oppression;

• Defend freedom of expression and cultural diversity, giving preference always to dialogue and listening without engaging in fanaticism, defamation and the rejection of others;

• Promote consumer behaviour that is responsible and development practices that respect all forms of life and preserve the balance of nature on the planet;

•   Contribute to the development of my community, with the full participation of women and respect for democratic principles, in order to create together new forms of solidarity.

This manifesto was created by a group of Nobel peace prize winners for the 50th Anniversary of the Universal Declaration of Human Rights.

UNESCO launched a campaign to collect signatures for the Manifesto, for the International Year for the Culture of Peace in 2000. Owing to the scope of the campaign, a website was created in order to collect the signatures: www.unesco.org/manifesto2000

The 75 million signatures collected in 2000 were presented to the United Nations General Assembly on 19 September 2000. Given the success achieved, it was decided to prolong the campaign throughout the International Decade for the Promotion of a Culture of Peace and Non-violence and Peace for the Children of the World (2001–2010).

Some personalities who express the universal values of non-fragmentation and interdependence

Roberto ASSAGIOLI
Sri AURABINDO
BAHAUDDIN
Gregory BATESON
Charles BAUDOIN
Siméon BEN YOCHAI
Henri BERGSON
William BLAKE
Jacob BOEHME
David BOHM
Niels BOHR
Richard Maurice BUCKE
Fritjof CAPRA
Maryse CHOISY
The DALAÏ LAMA
Thérèse D'AVILA
Marie-Madeleine DAVY
Pierre THEILHARD DE CHARDIN
Jean DE LA CROIX
Lanza DEL VASTO
Paul DE TARSE
Taisen DESHIMARU
Arnaud DESJARDINS
Eugen DREWERMANN
K. G. DURKHEIM
Master ECKHART

Albert EINSTEIN
Mircea ELIADE
Matthew FOX
Victor FRANKL
Erich FROMM
Michael GORBACHEV
Stanislav GROF
René GUENON
Georges Ivanovitch GURDJIEFF
Aldous HUXLEY
William JAMES
Carl Gustav JUNG
Emmanuel KANT
Arthur KOESTLER
KRISHNAMURTI
LAO TSEU
Jean-Yves LELOUP
Henri LE SAUX
LONGCHEMPA
Stephan LUPASCO
Ramana MARPA MAHARISHI
Abraham MASLOW
Thomas MERTON
MILAREPA
Jacob Lévy MORENO
Baba MUKTANANDA
OUSPANSKI

Fernando PESSOA
Karl PRIBRAM
Ilya PRIGOGINE
Baba RAM DASS
RAMAKRISHNA
Carl ROGERS
RUMI
Rupert SHELDRAKE
Baal SCHEM TOV
Albert SCHWEITZER

Rabindranâth TAGORE
THICH NHAT HANH
Chögyam TRUNGPA
Tartang TULKU
Ludwig VON BERTALANFY
Allan WATTS
Ken WILBER
Paramahansa YOGANANDA

among others . . .

UNIPAIX

Since its foundation in 1988, the International Holistic University of the City of Peace Foundation UNIPAIX in Brasilia has developed as a UNIPAIX network made up of units in the shape of 'campuses' (non-profit-making, democratic associations, organized in conformity with legal requirements and respecting the network's principles of action) and 'delegations' (recently created associations or ones in the process of being created, that are due to become 'campuses').

There were twenty-eight units including ten campuses and eighteen delegations on three continents in mid-2001. These units offer various courses and seminars including 'The Art of Living in Peace'.

For further details about their activities, you will find contact information for some below.

In Brazil

Unipaz
Fundaçáo Cidade de Paz
Caïxa Postal 19521
CEP 70001-970
Brasilia
Tel. : +5(0)61 380 18 85
Fax : +5(0)61 380 12 02
paz@tba.com.br
www.unipaz.com.br

In Portugal

Unipaz
Rue D. Pedro V.
n°60-1° Dto
Tel.: +351 21 34 78 236
unipaz@unipaz.pt
www.unipaz.pt

Unipaix Europe

19 Ave des Gobelins
F-75005 Paris
Tel.: +33(1)47 07 40 64
info@unipaix.org
www.unipaix.org

In Belgium

Unipaix Belgique
rue de Trou Renard 36
B-4870 Fraipont
Tel.: +32(0)87 46 21 80
unipaix@swing.be

In France

Unipaix France
13A rue St-Ouen-de-Pierrecourt
F-76100 Rouen
Tel.: 33(0)235 03 24 21
info@unipaix.org

The author

Pierre Weil was born in Strasbourg in the period between the two world wars.

As a child he found himself plunged into political conflicts between France and Germany as an inhabitant of Alsace. At the same time he was faced with inter-religious conflicts within his family, the members of which belonged to three different religions. These circumstances helped make him aware of the value of peace and the weight of boundaries at an early age.

Pierre Weil gained a Ph.D. in psychology at the University of Paris VII and studied under eminent psychologists and teachers such as Henri Wallon, André Rey and Jean Piaget. He went on to train as a psychotherapist with Igor Caruso, Jacob Lévy Moreno and Ancelin Schützenberger.

He took up a chair of social psychology at the Federal University of Belo Horizonte in Brazil and then took over the first chair of transpersonal psychology, a discipline he has pioneered.

He was invited by the Governor of Brasilia in 1986 to set up the City of Peace Foundation with the aim of founding the International Holistic University of Brasilia UNIPAIX in 1988, for which he is the director of studies. In this capacity he has elaborated a transdisciplinary programme for peace education, the basic seminar of which is 'The Art of Living in Peace'. This seminar has been given successfully in various countries around the world.

He has written a number of works, some of which have been translated into French, such as *L'Homme sans Frontières* and *Le Dernier Pourquoi*.

In 2000, Pierre Weil was awarded the Honorary Mention for the UNESCO Education for Peace prize by the Director-General, Koïchiro Matsuura.